From Cross to Cross

The musings of a Jewish boy riding his motorcycle through the Christian world.

by Lenny Mandel

10/3/01

JAMES. David –
oh! I didn't forget you Jax –

The book that I now
had – carry thin –
I've always enjoyed you.

love – Pops

FIRST EDITION
Copyright© 2005 by Lenny Mandel

10-Digit ISBN 1-59113-783-7
13-Digit ISBN 978-1-59113-783-2

All rights reserved. No part of this publication may be reproduced, stored in a retrieval system, or transmitted in any form or by any means, electronic, mechanical, recording or otherwise, without the prior written permission of the author.

Cover art-Lenny Mandel from a photo by Wulf Sonne

The story, "Protestant B, Not," is excerpted from This Jewish Life: Stories of Discovery, Connection and Joy, copyright 2003 by Debra B. Darvick. Used with permission of the author.

The excerpts from "Two," by Ron Elisha, used with permission of the author.

The excerpts from "One Hundred Gates," by Tuvia Tenenbom, are used with permission of the author.

The lyrics to "Friends (Travel On and In Peace My Brother) by Frank Fuchs and Andy Holiner, are used with permission of the authors.

The lyrics to "My Zeide," by Moshe Yess, are used with permission of the author.

WASN'T THAT A TIME by Lee Hays and Walter Lowenfels. Copyright 1957 (renewed) by SANGA MUSIC, INC. All rights reserved. Used by permission.

"You've Got To Be Carefully Taught" by Richard Rodgers and Oscar Hammerstein II. Copyright © 1949 by Richard Rodgers and Oscar Hammerstein II. Copyright Renewed WILLIAMSON MUSIC owner of publication and allied rights throughout the World. International Copyright Secured. All Rights Reserved. Used by Permission

Excerpts from NIGHT by Elie Wiesel, translated by Stella Rodway. Copyright © 1960 by MacGibbon & Kee. Copyright renewed ©1988 by The Collins Publishing Group. Reprinted by permission of Hill and Wang, a division of Farrar, Straus and Giroux, LLC.

Excerpts from Conversations With My Father and I'm Not Rappaport used with permission of the Estate of Herb Gardner

In My Life
Copyright 1965 (Renewed) Sony/ATV Tunes LLC. All rights administered by Sony/ATV Music Publishing, 8 Music Square West, Nashville, Tn 37203. All rights reserved. Used by permission.

Woodstock
Copyright 1973 Crazy Crow Music. All rights administered by Sony/ATV Music Publishing, 8 Music Square West, Nashville, TN 37203. All rights reserved. Used by permission.

ACKNOWLEDGEMENTS

To create this page correctly, I would have to list every person who shaped, and even those who mis-shaped, my life, so I'll just thank those who gave me input on the things I wrote, or the manner in which I wrote them, for this book.

My mom spent a couple of weeks at our home after rehab from hip replacement surgery. She sat down with the manuscript and when she finished looked at me and said; "Wow, it's a long book, but it gave me a lot of insight into things I never knew." We are still chuckling.

Kathy Ales
George Auerbach
Gary "cuda" Baronofsky
Robert Lash
Nedda Lash
Lotte Mandel
Shelly Mandel
Stacie Dale Mandel
Wayne Mandel
I. Dan Morrow
Fred Pierce
Michael J. Reimer
Harriet Turk
Arthur Weisel
Wayne Young
"The Peanut" Dylan Luke Mandel

My utmost gratitude to Seymour Turk without whose expertise and tireless help this piece would still be in a "Word" file on my computer.

Travel on, and in peace my brother.
Warm the faces not yet seen.
Leaving places, liking others,
living somewhere in between.

Be a stream a-gently flowing.
Weave your patterns 'cross the land.
Then stop that dream 'cause you know it's growing,
ever upward as you stand.

'Cause it's only to make a life for you,
only to wake you up to your life.
Picking a road following it on down to the end,
meeting new neighbors, greeting new friends.

Trains pull out just to leave you lonely,
faces fade of down the track.
You wave your arms goodbye, your head is thinking only,
wonderin' when you will be back.

So, take your time my brother and do your living,
any way the next road goes.
For one thing found in tomorrow's giving,
is that today just never knows.

Written by Frank Fuchs & Andy Holiner

"Be good and for your birthday I'll buy you a motorcycle!"

One of the many things a Jewish mother would never say.

Table of Contents

PROLOGUE XVII
CHAPTER 1 THE JOURNEY BEGINS HEADING TO
    GETTYSBURG 1
CHAPTER 2 THE JEWS AND THE CIVIL WAR 11
CHAPTER 3 MY FOLKS–MY THOUGHTS 15
CHAPTER 4 VIRGINIA AND THE LURAY CAVERNS 31
CHAPTER 5 DAY THREE THE BACK ROADS OF
    VIRGINIA 45
CHAPTER 6 THE SAME DAY NORTH CAROLINA 53
CHAPTER 7 SWASTIKAS THROUGHOUT MY LIFE 57
CHAPTER 8 PRELUDE TO THE RIDES 71
CHAPTER 9 NOVA SCOTIA 1996 77
CHAPTER 10 THE 2001 RIDE TO MONTREAL 83
CHAPTER 11 IN MONTREAL--STILL 2001 89
CHAPTER 12 STILL 2001--GOING BACK TO CAMP 97
CHAPTER 13 HEADIN' FOR ONTARIO–STILL 2001 103
CHAPTER 14 BOBBY AND NEDDA 109
CHAPTER 15 BLOWING ROCK, N.C. 111
CHAPTER 16 ASHEVILLE, NORTH CAROLINA DAYS
    THREE AND FOUR 115
CHAPTER 17 DAY FOUR MID-DAY 123
CHAPTER 18 DAY FIVE HEADING INTO TENNESSEE 137
CHAPTER 19 SAME DAY- MID AFTERNOON—
    HEADING TO DEALS GAP 151
CHAPTER 20 BARCELONA 1969 IN MY MIND 163
CHAPTER 21 STILL HEADING TO DEALS GAP,
    THINKING ABOUT MY DAD 171
CHAPTER 22 DEALS GAP '94 AND NOW 179
CHAPTER 23 JELLICO, TENNESSEE, HEADING TO
    KENTUCKY 187
CHAPTER 24 LEXINGTON KENTUCKY--HORSE
    COUNTRY 195

CHAPTER 25 DID DANIEL BOONE EVER MEET A
    RACIST?..205
CHAPTER 26 DAY SIX MID-DAY HEADING FOR WEST
    VIRGINIA 217
CHAPTER 27 EREV INDEPENDENCE DAY......................221
CHAPTER 28 JULY 4TH PENNSYLVANIA HERE WE
    COME 227
CHAPTER 29 MID-DAY DAY SEVEN- LENNY IS A BITCH
    DAY 233
CHAPTER 30 THE MORNING OF DAY EIGHT 237
CHAPTER 31 THE RIDE HOME, WHAT I WAS THEN &
    WHERE I AM NOW 247
EPILOGUE—INTO NEW JERSEY..257
GLOSSARY OF JEWISH TERMS...267
GLOSSARY OF BIKER TERMS 273

The Pope steps out onto the balustrade overlooking St. Peter's Square and begins to bless the people. Right in the middle of the benediction he sees a Hasidic Jew standing in the square in the middle of the throng, and stops.

The Pope points down at the Hasid: the Hasid points back up at the Pope. With that, the Pope turns on his heel, leaves the balustrade, goes down the stairs and out into the square. The Swiss Guard leads the way and the sea of people part to let them pass. The Pope walks up to the Hasid, puts his arm around the Jew's shoulders and whispers in his ear. The Jew nods, the Pope nods, turns and walks back inside.

"What the hell was that all about?" an Italian man standing next to the Hasid screamed. "I'm a devout Catholic, I pray the rosary three times a day. You're a Jew, what could the Pope have said to you? Why are you so important?" The Hasid shrugged his shoulders and after a few minutes, left.

The Italian thought about it and jumped into action. He went into town, bought a long black coat, a round black hat, a fake beard and fake sidelocks and the following week went to St. Peter's Square dressed like a Hasidic Jew.

Once again the Pope stepped out onto the balustrade overlooking St. Peter's Square and began to bless the people, and, once again, right in the middle of his benediction he saw the Hasidic Jew (the Italian dressed like the Jew) and stopped.

The Pope pointed down at the Hasid: the Hasid pointed back up at the Pope. Again the Pope turned on his heel, left the balustrade, went down the stairs and out into the square, and again the Swiss Guard led the way and the sea of people parted to let them pass.

Just as he had done the week before, the Pope walked up to the Hasid, put his arm around his shoulders and whispered in his ear: "Didn't I tell you last week to get the hell out of here?"

PROLOGUE

Why the hell would a Jewish kid ride a motorcycle anyway?"

It's a question I've been asked since 1965. It's as if it's not something a Jewish boy would do.

Ask a gentile and he'll just shrug his shoulders and wonder why you'd ask such a silly question. "Why wouldn't a Jew ride a motorcycle?" Ask a Jew and he'll look at you quizzically also wondering why you'd ask such a silly question. "Jews don't ride motorcycles, they're dangerous."

Buddy Hackett used to do a routine about when his wife asked him to go skiing.

"Jews don't ski," he said, "Jews play gin-rummy and say, Helen bring fruit."

"But you skied in the Catskills," she said.

"The Catskills?" he said, "those are little Jewish hills made out of sour cream. If you fall down they chop up a banana right where you land and you have lunch. You want to send me to gigantic Christian mountains that are shouting, c'mon Jew boy we're waiting for you."

I did plenty of things 'nice Jewish boys' didn't do. The running joke in my home was that I must have been adopted. I was paying to ride horses, drive a jeep, and shoot guns--(1) I definitely couldn't really be Jewish, (2) I could join the army and do it all and get paid at the same time.

Lenny Mandel

One of the reasons that I ride a motorcycle is Bob Schindler. A very large man, 6'5" tall and 265 lbs., Bob was a hard-hat diver in the Aleutian Islands during WWII. He was down more than a hundred feet when the Japanese sank his tender. Bob made his way to the surface, and despite orders from the United States Government not to pick up anybody in the water for fear it was a Japanese trap, some U.S. Navy ship picked him up. Sue got the telegram from the war department: "We regret to inform you…" while he was recuperating on some island in the Pacific.

Bob, who was a devout atheist, played chess with my dad, an observant Jew, all the time. They had some pretty interesting, and sometimes very heated conversations about G-D while they played.

He is the man who drove me to school for early morning prayers on the back of his Vespa. When we visited him in Florida, to my parents' chagrin and against my dad's wishes, he let me ride it. I was hooked.

It's been many years since I rode to elementary school on the back of that Vespa. More ironic is the fact that I rode to Yeshiva holding my skullcap tightly to my head. (It was then that I truly understood the reason men should carry bobby pins with them). I was twelve then, and knew that I would own a scoot as soon as I could. Six years later, I did. No matter what people said, "Jews don't ride motorcycles," or "You're an embarrassment to yourself and to your people," I felt alive on my ride.

Fast-forward twenty eight years, to the National H.O.G. Rally in Asheville, North Carolina.

Seven thousand bikers stood around before opening ceremonies when I arrived with a couple of

From Cross To Cross

members of my H.O.G. chapter. The others with me were not Jewish. I wore my Star of David Motorcycle Club T-shirt, the words encircling a large, blue six-pointed star.

People gawked, nudged each other, and pointed. One man asked me to bring him a beer and a Nazi helmet. I told him that I'd bring him the helmet, with the head of the guy who wore it, still inside.

These weren't locals or 1%ers; every biker there was a member of H.O.G.

Was my shirt offensive? I don't think so, but, like many of us who ride two wheels, I'm often horribly misunderstood.

The opening ceremonies ended, and as we headed out into the parking lot, I heard a woman screaming at her husband, "Look, look, look at that shirt!" I turned, anticipating an attack when she said, "C'mon Irving, look at the shirt!" I couldn't stop laughing, half out of relief that there wasn't going to be a brawl. She wanted to know where she could get the shirt, and she wasn't the only one who asked.

There are plenty of 'raisons d'etre' for a bike club, why not a Jewish club? My father rode a motorcycle in Vienna, until the day the Nazis marched in and took it away from him, and there was a Jewish bike club called Maccabee in Europe in the 30s. It, once again, recalls Shylock's speech in The Merchant of Venice ("hath not a Jew eyes ... if you tickle us do we not laugh...").

Suffice it to say that Jewish motorcycle clubs have all the same problems and go through all the same crap as every other motorcycle club. This includes what the press writes, and therefore the public's perception of us.

Lenny Mandel

Unlike our ancestors who rode horses out of necessity, we ride because we love it. Not unlike many of these ancestors, we think of ourselves as noble knights, riding into some foray with sword in hand, or rescuing damsels in distress astride our mounts.

That isn't the way it is anymore and, to tell the truth, I haven't seen a dragon since 'Dragon' Goldfarb cruised Kings Highway back in the 60's (he was a guy we used to hang out with) and he was too much fun to be with to slay.

So, how do we, 'The Knights of the Iron Horse' continue doing the good work of the days of yore? We go on myriad runs that support myriad charities. In truth, these are mostly happenings, the charities secondary to the event. Now far be it for me to think that there is anything wrong with happenings. On the contrary, I love 'em, hell, I was at Woodstock. They're great, they're exciting, they bring lots of fun people together, and they raise substantial sums of money for wonderful causes. But, it's not enough! In October 1999, the Chai (Hebrew for life) Riders—my club, which we jokingly refer to as Mel's Angels—was covered in an article published by The Forward, a 102-year old Yiddish newspaper. We rode up to New York's Catskill Mountains one Sunday in August. It was a back-roads ride, not unlike any other club ride, except that we had an unusual destination: a camp for children with either severe learning disabilities or Down's syndrome.

There were only thirteen or fourteen of us who braved the pouring rain for half the trip upstate and we rode into camp with no idea what to expect. We were directed through the camp to the basketball court, where we parked our bikes.

En masse, the campers began to move toward us. We quickly warned them that the bike's engines were hot and they'd have to wait a while until they could get closer to them.

With these over-active kids bouncing around, we talked about bikes and riding. They drew closer and closer, until we were finally engulfed. What sheer delight! I'm still smiling. These kids were all over our bikes and all over us.

Their conditions prohibited actual riding, but they donned our helmets, in some cases our leathers, and mounted up. Most of the kids had to be lifted onto the bikes, and hundreds of pictures were taken.

Have you ever seen the look on the faces of children who see something for the first time, something that is foreign to them or their environment? Have you ever seen the smile that lights up a face or the glow that remains?

Now picture children with Down's Syndrome, sitting on big old Harleys, wearing helmets, the children's arms stretched forward grasping (or trying to grasp) the handlebars.
Picture it!

Had we ridden in at night, the glow on the faces of these kids would've lit up the sky. We spent two or three hours at the camp. We left exhausted and exhilarated. The kids are still talking about it. You want to know something? So are we.

Lenny Mandel

What did the reporter say about the trip, after interviewing us? "They went to a camp for special children to show off their bikes."
What did he miss? Did he think we were on a jaunt and just happened upon this camp? We never would have expected this sort of misunderstanding from one of our own. Maybe he should have actually come up to the camp with us and not do an after-the-fact report. He had ridden with us once before in an attempt to uncover the mystery of the Jewish biker, but it seemed to have done little; his words were undoubtedly based on his preconceived notions of bikers in general. In any case we'll never know.

We have to try harder to make them see past the hooting and the hollering, past the screaming throttles and loud pipes and make them be a part of all the glorious things we do for these children. Make known the good work we do, and show that beyond our "Live To Ride, Ride To Live" motto (which we pronounce "Live To Ride, Ride To Eat") we also live by the words of William Shakespeare from Romeo and Juliet, "...the more I give to thee, the more I have..."

Chapter 1
The Journey Begins heading to Gettysburg

June 2003 was full of rain in the New York area. It broke a hundred-year record, so we were ecstatic when our eight-day motorcycle trip down South began with beautiful sunshine.

My wife Shelly and I were heading to Gettysburg, Pennsylvania, meeting old friends from Canada and riding the Blue Ridge Mountains through Southwestern North Carolina, Eastern Tennessee and Kentucky. It was a ride that would keep me thinking: bringing me back to my youth, my faith, my faith in my faith, my family and my beliefs.

You become one with everything around you when you're on a motorcycle; if it's raining, windy, sunny, hot or cold, you can't roll up the windows and escape—you either pull over or you just ride on. If your windshield is low, which ours is, some bugs miss it but don't miss you—trust me, getting whacked in the head by some bug at sixty-five miles an hour or so is not a joy. So there we were, boogying down the highway, bye, bye New Jersey, hello Pennsylvania, singing as we always do: it was a delight!

Lenny Mandel

It was early in our trip to Gettysburg when I saw the first billboard: "Do you have Christ in Your life?"

I have no idea how old I was when I first saw the sign: 'Believe on the Lord Jesus Christ and Thou Shalt be Saved.' The old BMT Brighton line went over the Manhattan Bridge and there was the sign, its letters as big as I'd ever seen. I turned to my mom and asked what it meant. "It has nothing to do with us, we don't believe in Jesus Christ," she said.

I saw that sign thousands of times, and when I went to High School I wondered about the grammar: Believe on? They must mean believe in! I wonder why no one's corrected this after all these years? Hey, it was a thought.

The farther we rode into Pennsylvania the more signs and the more billboards there were, and there were crosses. Little crosses, big crosses, white crosses, black crosses, some with flowers around the bases; everywhere I looked there was a cross, or so it seemed. The most predominant was three crosses together; I assumed that they represented 'The Father', 'The Son' and one for 'The Holy Spirit.'

The first morning of this year's trip was mostly route 78, and at highway speeds everything goes by in a rush. Sights and smells all seem to blend into one big blur.

Finally we got off and headed into the town of Gettysburg. There were more churches, more crosses and more signs. I wasn't afraid, I wasn't annoyed, I was overwhelmed.

From Cross To Cross

We pulled into the visitor's center and waited for Bob and Nedda and ten minutes later they pulled into the lot. We bought tickets for the bus tour of Gettysburg and walked across the street to the National Cemetery; it is solemn and quiet, and rightfully so.

There are hundreds of graves marked only with numbered small stones. These are many of the unknown dead; there's no telling how many rotted on the battlefield in the sweltering heat July first, second and third of 1863. Each section is laid out in an arc with a large stone at the head of the arc with the name of the State and the number of men buried there written on it. In the middle is a huge monument on the spot where Abe Lincoln delivered The Gettysburg Address.

A few years before this Bob Lash and I were riding back roads and, just by coincidence, ended up at West Point; that trip made me see Abraham Lincoln in a completely different light. We all know where he stood regarding slavery, but I never read, nor did I ever hear, anything that connected him and the Jews.

"HUA," (pronounced, HOO-aaaah), Rabbi Huerta said in a soft voice, "hua."

The Shul sits high on the side of a cliff, built into the rocks, overlooking the Hudson River. Strange place for the Shul, I thought. You can hardly see it. As a matter of fact if you didn't know that it was there, you'd miss it. It's a modern building with the Luchot HaBrit standing high and proud on its façade. That's what we spotted; that's what made us turn our bikes around and go up the hill to 'check it out.'

We walked in and headed toward the soulful sounds of a saxophone somewhere in the building.

Immediately to our left was a picture of Abraham Lincoln. How do we know that Abe Lincoln was Jewish? He was shot in the temple (sorry, I couldn't resist)! Neither Bob nor I gave that picture a second thought--maybe we should have.

There were lithographs by Chagall on the wall, and many posters of Jewish women who had made stunning contributions to the world.

We walked down a corridor, hearing the sax getting louder, and at the end of the corridor there he was. The man playing the sax had to be six foot five and two hundred seventy five pounds. He was in the Synagogue, standing on the Bimah, his music resting on the shtender, playing the saxophone. We stood in the doorway silently waiting for him to finish and when he did, he looked up and we all nodded hello. There was no way we'd have known who he was: Hispanic looking with dark features, salt and pepper hair peeking out from under a black beret perched on his head and his name--Huerta.

He extended his hand. "Huerta," he said, "Rabbi Carlos Huerta."

"You're the Rabbi here?" I asked.

"Hua," he said in a soft voice, and I was sure that he wasn't talking about a girl standing on the corner of Bay Parkway and 86th Street, in Brooklyn snapping her gum, "hua."

"Hi, I'm Cantor Lenny Mandel from Congregation B'nai Israel in Emerson New Jersey," I said, and then introduced my friend Bobby, a barrister from Toronto, Ontario.

"Hua," he said again.

From Cross To Cross

What began as a beautiful Friday morning with my old friend Bobby and me just going for a motorcycle ride through the back roads of Northern New Jersey and lower New York State ended up as a glorious learning experience.

Bobby and his wife Nedda, who ride with YOW (Yids on Wheels) up in Toronto, came down for a visit, and, as I have two bikes, he brought riding gear down with him and we boogied. The section of route 513 (a one lane road in each direction) we rode is 'light-free' for twelve miles and we continued past route 23, up Union Valley Road to West Milford, New Jersey. From there we rode around Greenwood Lake, New Jersey and then New York, up one of the 17's through Harriman State Park and through the Seven Lakes Road.

Bobby rode my BMW K1200RS, while I was on my Harley Davidson FLHS and we rode, whipping through those roads, ending up on Route 6 when I saw the signpost. We turned, as the sign directed, and continued on an eleven-mile jaunt through military encampments until we got to a concrete barricade.
The guard, a ranger sergeant carrying a sub-machine gun, asked us for our licenses. Bob was a bit slow to find his.

"C'mon, c'mon," the now impatient soldier said, "show me your driver's license or a military I.D. card." He already had mine and he prodded Bob again.
Bobby looked up at him, and screamed, "I'm a G-D damn ally. For G-D's sake, I'm a Canadian. Do you want to see my health card?" We thought that was pretty funny (sub-machine gun notwithstanding). He finally found his license and the sergeant let us on the base.

Lenny Mandel

We were at West Point, The United States Military Academy, and Rabbi Huerta stood on the Bimah of the Synagogue in camouflage fatigues, pants bloused into spit shined combat boots, a gold leaf on each lapel which signified his rank-major, and on his beret the insignia of a Jewish Chaplain--the Tablets that Moses brought down with him from Mount Sinai. It was splendiferous and what made it even more so was the fact that the symbol for each of the ten on his beret was done with the letters of the Aleph Bet (the Hebrew alphabet).

You can see the Cadet Chapel (a West Point landmark building and the Christian House of Worship)) the minute you ride in to 'The Point'; it has been in many movies, and stands overlooking the Hudson River. It's one heck of a view.

The interior of the chapel is, well, the interior of a chapel. Magnificent stained glass, huge pipes from the organ and, what looks like one hundred yards of pews. There was a small sign that asked all visitors to say a prayer to G-D and as we walked up the side aisle I said one of the early morning, opening, blessings that is chanted every day in traditional Synagogues. The acoustics are incredible and I suppressed an overwhelming desire to sing out a rousing 'hi ge diggy di,' or 'Etz Chayim He.'

I asked Bob where he thought the Jewish cadets prayed (not knowing that he was thinking the exact thoughts) and we looked in all the small side rooms, concurring that there must be some catacomb where they allow 'Members of the Tribe' to worship their G-D.

We left the chapel, mounted our bikes and headed down toward the Hudson River when I saw the tablets.

Perched on a hill above the Cadet Chapel were the Ten Commandments, written in Hebrew. We turned around, rode up the hill and we were at the Shul. The Shul. You can't imagine what we felt, and Rabbi Huerta was overjoyed to be able to show us around.

"I was born in Brooklyn," he said as we walked. "I'm sure that my name threw you off, but I am Sephardic. As a matter of fact I was ordained in Jerusalem and I'm an observant Jew in this setting of egalitarianism." I couldn't help but think how incredible that was.

"There are two refrigerators, sinks and microwaves--one each for dairy and the other for meat," he continued as we walked, and he gleefully showed us the back yard, cut out of the side of the cliff, where they build a Sukkah every year and will have their first wedding soon.

"There are forty one hundred cadets at West Point," he said, "and thirty five of them are Jewish."
"Forty one hundred?" Bob asked.
"It's the number mandated by Congress," he replied, "and there are about sixty five Cadre, staff and their families here as well."

The Shul was funded and built by some Jewish Cadets who graduated West Point in the 50s, became very successful, and wanted to make sure that there was a House of Worship for Jews to pray in while students at 'The Point.' They didn't want the Jewish cadets relegated to some room, and to their delight the Shul is 'Standing Room Only' on Rosh Hashanah and Yom Kippur.

It's a thrill to see the names, most of them famous, household names: Eisenhower Hall, The Patton and MacArthur monuments, Doubleday Field and, of course, the Lichtenberg Tennis Center (Herb (USMA '55) Lichtenberg and Alan (USMA '51) Lichtenberg). Unbeknownst to most, they also funded the floor and the new sound systems in the Catholic Church and 'The Cadet Chapel.'

It was a wonderful day but Rabbi Huerta had to go teach a Hebrew class where, he told us, "half of the students aren't Jewish,' so we headed for the door. I told him that we'd like to come up one Erev Shabbat to daven with them.

"Hua," he said, 'hua," which means H-heard, U-understood, A-acknowledged.

Abe Lincoln's picture? Well, 'honest Abe' certainly was not a Member of the Tribe, no sireee. He was however, the President who abolished the military law that in order to be a Chaplain in the military one had to be of good Christian character.

Thanks Abe, you lived up to your namesake, our father Abraham.

As important as Abraham Lincoln was to the United States, he made a difference in equality on many levels: this one heretofore unknown to me.

As I stood looking up at Lincoln's monument in Gettysburg, I thought about the trip to 'The Point' and a smile crossed my lips. I wondered if any of the boys who died here had ever even seen a Jew. The fact that they hated Jews was automatic and probably for no real reason.

A song from Rodgers and Hammerstein's South Pacific played in my head. This song was written, deleted, put back in and deleted again. Mr. Rodgers and Mr. Hammerstein had to make a choice as to the offensive nature of the song although it wasn't offensive: it was pointed, truthful, and way ahead of its time. There was fear that it would cause riots and bad sentiment toward the play. They made the choice to keep it in and to hell with those who it pissed off. I sang under my breath:

> You've got to be taught to hate and fear.
> You've got to be taught from year to year.
> It's got to be drummed in your dear little ear.
> You've got to be carefully taught.
>
> You've got to be taught to be afraid
> Of people whose eyes are oddly made,
> And people whose skin is a different shade.
> You've got to be carefully taught.
>
> You've got to be taught before it's too late,
> before you are six or seven or eight,
> to hate all the people your relatives hate.
> You've got to be carefully taught.

It was time to take the tour of the battlefields.

I was never a big history buff; my teachers taught it without flair, without energy, and without excitement. Our guide here was great, and the battle came alive as he spoke: Cemetery Hill, Cemetery Ridge, Seminary Ridge, Little Round Top, The Peach Orchard, Pickett's charge. The feelings on the battlefield were palpable.

I thought of this insanity and an old folk song, Two Brothers, ran through my head.

The two brothers were us, brothers from the North in blue and brothers from the South in gray. I picture them young, very alive, and each marching under a gorgeous blue sky to, well they never knew where to. The end of the song speaks volumes, again, in color. The soldiers had wives, girlfriends and mothers waiting for them to come home from the war. The colors they wore represented their feelings; they wore bright colors if their boys were coming back alive and if not they wore black.

That's the way I remember it and I hadn't thought of that song for more than thirty years, or the lines from Lee Hayes' Wasn't That a Time.

> ...Brave men who died at Gettysburg
> Now lie in soldier's graves,
> But there they stemmed the slavery tide...

We stood where the Confederate army began its charge, where they shelled the Bluecoats for hours and heard their cries. Most of these soldiers were kids--flag bearers and buglers as young as eight and ten. It was a crime, a great tragedy, a travesty, but most certainly a crime.

I don't remember where I saw it, heard it, or read it, but I thought about these words:

"It is the soldier, not the reporter, who has given us the freedom of the press. It is the soldier, not the poet, who has given us the freedom of speech. It is the soldier, not the campus organizer, who gives us the freedom to demonstrate. It is the soldier who salutes the flag, who serves beneath the flag, and whose coffin is draped by the flag, who allows the protester to burn the flag." Freedom is NOT Free!

So where were the Jews during the Civil War? Fighting along with everybody else!

Chapter 2
The Jews and The Civil War

At our Passover Seder we add the story of a Jewish soldier, fighting with the Union army during the Civil War, who wanted to make a Seder. It's something I'd never thought about before, and why would I wonder about celebrating Jewish Holidays while in the army during the Civil War? I know that my dad held his Seder while fighting with the American Army in Europe during WWII, why wouldn't it have been the same in the 1860s? It would be; it was.

PASSOVER— A REMINISCENCE OF THE WAR
by J.A. Joel, "The Jewish Messenger", April 1866

"In the commencement of the war of 1861, I enlisted from Cleveland, Ohio, in the Union cause, to the Government of the United States, and became attached to the 23rd Regiment, one of the first sent from the "Buckeye State." Our destination was West Virginia—a portion of the wildest and most mountainous region of that State, well adapted for the guerrillas who infested that part, and caused such trouble to our pickets all through the war.

After an arduous march of several hundred miles through Clarksburgh, Weston, Sommerville, and several other places of less note, which have become famous during the war, we encountered on the 10th of September, 1861, at Carnifax Ferry, the forces under the rebel Gen. Floyd. After this, we were ordered to take up our position at the foot of Sewell Mountain, and we remained there until we marched to the village of Fayette, to take it, and to establish there our Winter-quarters, having again routed Gen. Floyd and his forces.

While lying there, our camp duties were not of an arduous character, and being apprised of the approaching Feast of Passover, twenty of my comrades and co-religionists belonging to the Regiment, united in a request to our commanding officer for relief from duty, in order that we might keep the holy days, which he readily acceded to. The first point was gained, and, as the Paymaster had lately visited the Regiment, he had left us plenty of greenbacks.

Our next business was to find some suitable person to proceed to Cincinnati, Ohio, to buy us matzos. Our sutler being a co-religionist and going home to that city, readily undertook to send them. We were anxiously awaiting to receive our matzos and about the middle of the morning of Passover a supply train arrived in camp, and to our delight seven barrels of Matzos. On opening them, we were surprised and pleased to find that our thoughtful sutler had enclosed two Haggadahs and prayer-books. We were now able to keep the seder nights, if we could only obtain the other requisites for that occasion. We held a consultation and decided to send parties to forage in the country while a party stayed to build a log hut for the services.

About the middle of the afternoon the foragers arrived, having been quite successful. We obtained two kegs of cider, a lamb, several chickens and some eggs. Horseradish or parsley we could not obtain, but in lieu we found a weed, whose bitterness, I apprehend, exceeded anything our forefathers "enjoyed".

We were still in a great quandary; we were like the man who drew the elephant in the lottery. We had the lamb, but did not know what part was to represent it at the table; but Yankee ingenuity prevailed, and it was decided to cook the whole and put it on the table, then we could dine off it, and be sure we had the right part.

The necessaries for the choroutzes we could not obtain, so we got a brick which, rather hard to digest, reminded us, by looking at it, for what purpose it was intended.

At dark we had all prepared, and were ready to commence the service. There being no Rabbi present, I was selected to read the services, which I commenced by asking the blessing of the Almighty on the food before us, and to preserve our lives from danger.

The ceremonies were passing off very nicely, until we arrived at the part where the bitter herb was to be taken. We all had a large portion of the herb ready to eat at the moment I said the blessing; each ate his portion, when horrors! What a scene ensued in our little congregation, it is impossible for my pen to describe. The herb was very bitter and very fiery like Cayenne pepper, and excited our thirst to such a degree, that we forgot the law authorizing us to drink only four cups, and the consequence was we drank up all the cider.

Those that drank the more freely became excited, and one thought he was Moses, another Aaron, and one had the audacity to call himself Pharaoh. The consequence was a skirmish, with nobody hurt, only Moses, Aaron and Pharaoh, had to be carried to the camp, and there left in the arms of Morpheus.

This slight incident did not take away our appetite, and, after doing justice to our lamb, chickens and eggs, we resumed the second portion of the service without anything occurring worthy of note. There, in the wild woods of West Virginia, away from home and friends, we consecrated and offered up to the ever-loving G-D of Israel our prayers and sacrifices.

I doubt whether the spirits of our forefathers, had they been looking down on us standing there with our arms by our side ready for an attack, faithful to our G-d and our cause, would have imagined themselves amongst mortals, enacting this commemoration of the scene that transpired in Egypt.

To celebrate at a time like that. To show the world that even in times of great stress and under the worst possible circumstances we show, honor, respect and courage."

Tons of thoughts swirled through my head as the first day of our ride was coming to a close. We got back on our bikes, each reliving the battles we'd just 'seen' through the eyes of our guides and rode south out of Gettysburg. We spent the night in Frederick, Maryland, and the next morning turned our bikes southwest heading for Luray Caverns via the northernmost point of The Blue Ridge Parkway: Skyline Drive.

CHAPTER 3
My Folks–My Thoughts

I don't wonder why my thoughts, be they regarding my Judaism or the way things effect my life, run through my brain. I know.

I am the first generation son of two lucky escapees from Hitler's clutches, growing up in a predominantly Irish/Italian neighborhood. I went to a Yeshiva, wore a yarmulke, and although there were plenty of other Jewish kids around they, for the most part, went to public school, were secular Jews (or as I called them 'revolving door Jews'—in Rosh Hashanah and out Yom Kippur) and their parents were all born here. This wasn't true of many of our Catholic neighbors who spoke with thick brogues or heavy Italian accents.

My mom had a German accent, slight but definitely there.

The youngest of five children born in Baden-Baden, Germany, she was the spoiled brat. Her three oldest siblings were out of the house when she was growing up: medical school, nursing school, and gymnasium (High School in Germany) so it was only the two youngest, she and her brother, who grew up together. Wherever he went she wanted to tag-along; she must have been a real pain in his tuchas.

Lenny Mandel

By the time Hitler came to power, mom had already finished gymnasium and had a teaching certificate. Two SS came to the door one night. They told my grandfather to pack a bag and come. They asked about my uncles and my Grandmother said: "You'll never get my sons, they are in America already." It was a lie; one was a Doctor in Frankfurt, the other studying to be a Hazan, in Berlin: it didn't really matter, they weren't there.

They took my grandfather, along with the entire town's male, Jewish population, marched them through town and into a Synagogue (the Holocaust Museum in Washington, D.C. has the film and we can see him in it). The Nazis then locked the doors and set the Synagogue on fire. Either the doors broke open or someone on the outside pried off the wooden planks holding them shut, but my grandfather escaped. He ran home and announced: "We've got to leave, they're going to kill us all."

Just as they had escaped Ukraine in the early 1900s and fled to Germany, they were going to be on the move again.

My dad was born in a small town in Galicia, the youngest of three boys. My zeide was a Hasid of the Belzer Rebbe; he had a long white beard, payes and all the rest that goes with it.

The family moved to Vienna when my dad was three or four years old and the first time a teacher yanked on my father's payes, he cut them off himself.
Believe me, my father was a vantz of the first order. He played professional soccer on The Hakoah Wien, a world championship team, and when his dad found out, he hid his cleats. My father played anyway--barefoot--and my

From Cross To Cross

bubby knew it was smarter to let him wear his cleats than to play without them.

He was a dancer, loved to play billiards and cards and strayed from the path of Orthodox Judaism. He rode a motorcycle, and when the Nazis marched into Vienna they walked into his parents' apartment, and arrested him.

He escaped, fled to Hamburg, Germany and got on a boat to New York. Three years later he was drafted into the army and after escaping the Nazis, was sent back to Europe to fight with the American army. He and his unit liberated Dachau, Hitler's medical experimentation and extermination camp. It could have been him; any one of those skeletons could have been my dad.

As my dad walked from person to person, one of the many skeletons motioned to him to come over and asked if my dad spoke Yiddish--he did. He held this man in his arms and was told that when the Nazis came into this man's town he buried a Torah, so that they couldn't destroy it. He told my father where it was buried and made him promise that he'd make sure that it was retrieved. My dad promised, the man smiled and died in his arms. It's an image that has always haunted me and does to this day.

I have, what I call, 'first generation syndrome'. I wanted to shed any connection to 'the other side' and look, walk, talk, and live like an American.

I played the violin from the time I was six and my mom would lean out the window and shout: "Leonard (my mother still calls me Leonard, and my dad would only call me Leonard when he was pissed off at me), come up and practice your violin." It was beyond embarrassing.

The violin, and the opera, and ballet were cultures that I didn't want. I wanted to play baseball, and football. I wanted to go fishing on the party boats in Sheepshead Bay like all of my gentile and non-observant Jewish friends did.

When I'd ask my dad to have a catch with me he'd flip the ball to me with his toes. Instead of realizing what an incredible skill that was, it embarrassed me to death.

Every Yom Kippur, while sitting in Shul, my father would sing out: La da da dee da da da da ladada la da, as loud as he could, interrupting the Hazan's davening. I would cringe and slump lower in my seat as I nudged him with my elbow, or I'd walk out of Shul.

I was ashamed. The holiest day of the year and my dad is interfering with the Cantor's pleas for us, his Congregation, so that G-D would be merciful and seal us in the book of life for the upcoming year.

Do you know the famous chant: "wa tashma kayam?" Do you? Close your eyes and repeat it over and over, faster and faster. I know you get it now and probably have big smiles on your faces. The Hazan has been fasting, just as we have, and is using his voice for hours praying for us from the Bimah. What my dad was doing was giving him a break, a chance to catch his breath, a chance to swallow and maybe get some moisture into his parched throat and on his vocal folds (mistakenly called vocal chords). I really appreciate that now that I am a Hazan myself.

Wa tashma kaywas! No, not really, I was just young, embarrassed and uninformed.

My parents were from two cultures so different from each other that they could've been from separate planets.

From Cross To Cross

You think that men are from Mars and women are from Venus? Try growing up with a Galitzianer father and a Litvak mother. Although both were observant Jews, they each manifested their behavior toward me, where they stood on Judaism, very differently.

My dad's gig was laissez-faire and I never knew if it was real or if he was just letting my mother be the 'bad guy.' Stuff like: "where are your tzitzis, or did you daven this morning," were questions he liked to ask. On the other hand my mother would preface everything with: "Your father will be very upset if..."

I think that the driving force to keep me on the path of observance though, was my mom. Don't get me wrong, if my father came home and wanted to hear what I'd learned in Yeshiva that day, I'd better have known my stuff.

I didn't go to public school; I went to a Yeshiva, a Jewish parochial school.

> *Morris Goldberg didn't know what to do with his son Abie. He was a terror in school. He was thrown out of Yeshiva after two days, public school after four days, prep school after three days and military school after eight days. With no other options open Morris enrolled Abie in the local Catholic school.*
> *A month went by and Morris got a call from the Mother Superior to come to school; it was a call he'd been expecting for weeks.*
> *The Mother Superior was ecstatic. "Mr. Goldberg," she said, "Abie is a model student, straight A's. I wish all of our students were like him."*

> *Morris, perplexed, grabbed Abie by the ear and dragged him through the nearest doorway—it led into the Church, "What's this," he said "I sent you to every school under the sun and you were thrown out within a week, what's so special about this place?"*
> *Abie turned his dad around, pointed up at the crucifix and said; "Are you kidding, dad, I wouldn't dare mess up here, in this place they mean business."*

In Yeshiva we studied Hebrew and all of our Jewish studies from eight in the morning until noon and secular studies from 12:30 to 4:30. My Yeshiva, The Yeshiva of Flatbush was my elementary school life from September of 1952 until I graduated in June of 1960. Although it was an Orthodox Yeshiva they taught Hebrew, the language of our forefathers and not Yiddish, the language of the Shtetl. Yiddish was used as a secret language, in my home anyway. The irony of 'Yiddish-the secret language' thing is that no self-respecting German Jew ever lowered himself to speak Yiddish. Absolutely never: Yiddish was the language of the Polish/Eastern European Jew, and the German Jew was far too cultured for that—Oh yeah, far too cultured.

When my dad got home from work he always wanted to know what I'd learned that day in school. I would read the Hebrew text and then he'd close whatever book I was reading and ask me to explain it to him. I did it, but my explanations were also in Hebrew. It used to piss him off as he wanted to hear the explanation in Yiddish: the way he was taught growing up. In most Orthodox

From Cross To Cross

Yeshivas students learned to translate Hebrew, the language of the Torah and of the prayer books into Yiddish, the language of the Jews (Yiddish, not Jewish-- there is no language: Jewish).

He even went up to school one day to find out why I couldn't translate into Yiddish. The principal told him that if that's what he wanted, he chose the wrong Yeshiva. It was a wonderful school and my parents decided to let it go.

Having grown up in an observant home, there would never have been a choice as to what type of school I would go to, and many of the Catholic kids in the neighborhood went to Saint Brendan's. Why shouldn't I have gone to a Yeshiva? Most of the Jewish kids in the neighborhood came from non-observant homes, with very little connection to Orthodox Judaism, so they went to public school.

I don't remember much of the first or second grades except that my teachers were sweet and that they loved me. In the third grade my life--at least my school life--was turned upside down. Third grade was my downfall.

My Hebrew teacher, Mrs. Yaffa Eliach (today, a world renowned author and lecturer on The Holocaust), accused me of all kinds of behavior problems. Even though these accusations weren't true, she had me removed from the Aleph class: the class with the top students. I was relegated to the Gimmel class with the slowest kids in the grade.

True, I was the class clown and one day Mrs. Eliach pushed me down into my seat with such force that my head hit the metal chalk-holder and I was sent to the hospital for stitches. That notwithstanding, this was a world that I didn't want to be a part of, and a world that didn't want me either. I don't mean the world of Judaism; I mean the strict world of an orthodox Yeshiva where one rarely questioned. I did nothing but question.

So there I was, without a doubt the brightest kid in the class with the slowest kids; it was a joke, all A's in schoolwork, all U's (unsatisfactory) in conduct. Once relegated to the dungeon of intellect or the lack thereof, at the school, I knew that I wasn't going to continue past the eighth grade.

I ran a lot, too, while growing up, and I wasn't on the track team, or getting into shape for a marathon. No, I was a chubby Jewish kid trying to get away from the older, Christian kids--it rarely worked. I was a Christ killer: that's what they always screamed at me although I never knew how that could've possibly been true. My Catholic friends, and specifically those who weren't my friends, whether they went to Parochial school or only Catechism classes, all knew it.

They thought that I had the 'Jewish Answers' because I always wore a Yarmulke, which the other Jewish kids in the neighborhood didn't. This 'beanie' didn't stay on long after school hours because the older kids, 'The Avenue M Boys' or 'The Golden Guineas,' didn't feel that talking to me or hanging out with me was a cool thing to do. Naaah, kicking the shit out of me, or just scaring the shit out of me making me think that they were going to kick the shit out of me, was much more fun.

I sort of felt like Nat Moyer in Herb Gardner's I'm Not Rappaport when he is accosted by a street smart Irish

From Cross To Cross

kid. "Take it easy, I don't fight with Irish kids. I know the same thing now that I knew 65 years ago: don't fight with an Irish kid."

I knew not to fight? No, I couldn't fight, and it was many years before I raised my hands and actually threw punches. Wrestling was an entirely different thing.

Ostensibly you'd end up on the ground in a headlock, or giving a headlock to the other kid and one of you giving up. You could get hurt, but you couldn't get mangled. It was punches that could shatter teeth, or break a nose or end up with someone getting stitches in the head that scared me. I was a 'chubby' kid so not only didn't I fight, I couldn't outrun those bastards.

It must have amazed my mother how many times I 'tripped getting off the school bus,' all the days I came home with the knees in my pants ripped. Oh, well.

I took a bicycle ride down Ocean Avenue one day and ended up in a strange neighborhood. From out of nowhere three kids, also on bikes, chased me and we ended up in a schoolyard, where they cornered me. Each one had a canvas bag hanging over the handlebars of his Schwinn bicycle, with the words Journal American printed on it.

My parents read three papers a day; my dad read The Post and The Mirror and my mom read The Herald Tribune. The Journal American was never read in Jewish homes (don't ask me why).

I decided to ride through them and get away before they beat the crap out of me. They jammed their tires into my front wheel and that was it, I was going to get hurt.

I felt tears on my face and heard one kid say; "Hey, he's crying. What're you crying for we're not gonna hurt you. We were just trying to scare you." They did.

One of the others asked what Church I went to; I was silent. "He's Jewish," the third kid said, "Hey, kid, are you Jewish?" I nodded yes, I was terrified.

"Hey, it's alright," they said. "Here, have a newspaper. Do you want a newspaper?"

The only word I spoke was "no", they apologized, turned their bikes around and rode out of the yard.

Hell, what would I have done with The Journal American; no one I knew read it.

I didn't have to think very hard about why I felt trepidation when out of my element. It was the stories of the Nazis, and the pogroms all over Eastern Europe, Russia and the Ukraine that I heard from my parents and many of their friends. It was the memories of all the generations of Jews who were beaten, raped, robbed and burned at the stake for practicing the heretical religion, Judaism, which flooded my mind when I was surrounded by those boys. It's an interesting insanity believing in a religion that you get beaten and even killed for, by the very people who say that they believe in G-D and the Ten Commandments He handed down. I wondered where they learned all this hatred when their religion preaches love!

Don't think for a moment that my life growing up was all running and ducking, not even close. We had plenty of fun growing up. Brooklyn had its own games (all inner city kids probably played many of them) and they were a huge part of my childhood.

From Cross To Cross

There wasn't much grass so most of our games were played in the street, on the sidewalk and in the park (these were playgrounds on concrete) and, as none of our families had much money, our games were played with minimal equipment; a rubber ball was number one. As a matter of fact ninety five percent of our games required nothing else. The rubber ball of choice was a Spalding—we called it a 'spaldeen.'

Let me relate a cute story involving the name of our rubber ball of choice. In 1997 I starred in "Fiddler on the Roof," at the Tri-State Center for the Arts in Pine Plains, N.Y. and I was introduced to one of the members of the board whose surname was Spalding. I turned to him and said: "Spalding, wow, I used to play with your balls when I was a kid." It was an old one, but one that we used all the time growing up. The laugh was on me; he was the grandson of the founder of the company.

So there we'd be late in the day, playing stickball on East 17th Street. Eventually one of the kids' moms would scream from the fifth floor--"Where's my broom handle?" There couldn't be a game if one of us didn't unscrew the broom and take the handle to use as a bat. I remember when you had to cut off the handle, and that was the cause of many a spanking, no, a spanking and a half. Grounded? Being put in 'time out?' No such punishments existed when we were growing up. A good whack on your backside worked wonders.

Not all the cops were fond of our street games either, and many would chase us away when they drove around on patrol. The nastier ones would stop and take our sticks--our moms' sticks. That was cause for great trepidation: To go back upstairs without your mom's broom-handle? Whew!

Stickball was great as were punch ball and slap ball but you needed a bunch of kids to play and there weren't always a bunch of kids around when you needed them. Not to worry, there were plenty of games that two or three kids could play with only a spaldeen; well, a spaldeen and a wall, a sidewalk, a curb or the stoop of one of the one-family homes on the block. As a matter of fact, there were lots of these games that you could play alone by playing against yourself: making believe that you were the other player as well. The youth of today have replaced these wonderfully creative physical activities with television and computer games.

We played handball, king-queen, 'I declare war' and 'catch-a-fly's-up' all with just a ball and a wall. Stoopball was played with the ball and a stoop (duh!). Box ball, box baseball, corners, and hit the penny were played with a ball and the boxes that are always cut into the sidewalk. It was amazing what a couple of kids a spaldeen and some imagination could come up with.

We didn't play marbles much but we flipped cards and played Skelly, a game that very few people I've talked with ever heard of, outside of Brooklyn, of course.
The playing area was usually in the street, and the 'board' was drawn onto the blacktop with chalk. It was another game that required no equipment other than a bottle-cap and the ability to flick it with your finger around the board.

There was a playground with swings, a jungle gym, a seesaw, a couple of walls and a basketball court, but the older kids usually had the court.

From Cross To Cross

We wanted to play one day, and the rule was simple. You could 'challenge' for the court, and your team would play the next game. If you won you continued, if not you were back on the sidelines. The older kids ignored us and rather than fighting and getting our asses kicked the younger guys figured we'd play something else until they left. Not I. Phillip Goldberg and I found a small branch on the ground (yes, a tree does grow in Brooklyn) with a hollow end, and we stuffed a couple of firecrackers in it. He shielded me from their sight as I lit the fuses, and threw the stick at them onto the court. One of the older kids was about to pick it up and throw it back at us when it exploded. I never ran so fast in my life. It took them a few days, but the next time they saw me I paid for that stunt. All the same, it was definitely worth it.

There was nothing like growing up in Brooklyn in the 50s and 60s. It was safe, and if it wasn't, nobody knew about it. We'd ride the subway at all hours of the night with alacrity. We'd shoot down to Coney Island and, if we had money, we'd ride the merry-go-round, the Ferris wheel, one of the roller coasters, the whip, the loop de loop, bumper cars, or, we'd go into Steeplechase Park If we didn't have money we'd just hang out on the boardwalk or on the beach.

Of course there were the beaches: Manhattan Beach, Brighton Beach and Coney Island Beach. Polluted water? What was that?

That was back then, back in the 50s when things were simpler. Here, on this trip, I was an adult, A Jewish adult, and all the road signs, all the Churches and all the crosses on this trip constantly reminded me that I was a 'stranger' here: a stranger in my own land.

Lenny Mandel

I started to think again about Christianity's beginning and wondered: "if there are so many Christians and so few Jews, maybe they are right." I laughed and spat, a throwback to warding off the evil eye, thinking that if I say something and G-D was listening (and doesn't He always) and found it offensive, the spitting would let him know that I was only kidding. We wouldn't want to incur His wrath, now would we?

It's interesting how we keep referring to G-D as He. A buddy of mine, Michael Greer, wears a button on which is written: "G-D is coming and SHE is PISSED."

Christians do not want you to incur G-D's wrath, so they constantly proselytize. Who knows what might happen to you if you didn't take Christ into your heart?

A few years earlier, I'd come home from work and was greeted on my front lawn by two nicely dressed young men. They asked if I'd accepted Jesus as my personal savior.

I told them I was too busy for them as I was changing to get to an appointment (it was the truth). They asked again and I said: "no, I don't believe that Jesus was any more than an ordinary man who walked the earth a couple of thousand years ago." As we stood in my doorway they told me that I'd be damned and spend eternity in Hell.

I said that there were only two things in life you had to worry about--either you were healthy or you were sick. If you were healthy there was nothing to worry about and if you were sick there were only two things to worry about--either you'd live or you'd die. If you lived, there would be nothing to worry about and if you died there were only two things to worry about--either you'd go to Heaven or you'd go to Hell. If you went to Heaven there was nothing to worry about, and if you went to Hell you'd be so busy hanging out with your friends there'd be no time to worry. They didn't find this amusing; I did!

 I refused their offer of The Book of Mormon, aaah yes, I neglected to tell you that these weren't J W's (Jehovah Witnesses). They were L.D.S's (Mormons- The Church of Latter Day Saints). It was the first time I ever was proselytized by anyone other than J.Ws. By this time I'd had enough, I was tired, I was late and I wanted them gone. So I made the following statement about being saved and taking Jesus as my personal savior.

 "First of all," I said, "I am a Jewish Clergyman. I believe that when I die, if Jesus is really G-D's son, which he isn't, at least not any more than we all are G-D's children, he will have no choice but to greet me with open arms and welcome me into the heavenly kingdom. Here's the deal," I continued. "G-D, not his progeny, wrote the Ten Commandments, and handed them to Moses on Mt. Sinai. The Fifth Commandment reads: Honor Thy Father and Thy Mother. That is what I did my whole life; I followed their Judaic teachings as set down by G-D himself. If Jesus were to turn me away then he is going against what his Father wrote, and it's not like he had an ordinary Father. Nope, he had the Big Guy as his Father, no?"

 "If on the other hand," I wasn't done, and wasn't giving them any shot to interject, "he acknowledges the fact that I kept the commandments as originally written, and he is a truly benevolent savior, he will understand,

and welcome me. If you think that because I haven't accepted him during my days on Earth that he won't accept me when I get to Judgment Day, and I believe that there is going to be a Judgment Day, then you are without faith. Excuse me," I said.

I closed the door, changed my clothing, got on my motorcycle and went to my meeting. I laughed, thinking about the meeting and the looks on their faces when I said goodbye.

All through my life Jehovah's Witnesses have knocked on my door. I didn't know much about them except that they were pretty annoying. They would leave pamphlets, I never said no, and when my parents came home there was more stuff to throw into the incinerator. They were like telemarketers on foot and no less annoying than the phone calls we get these days which, for some strange reason, are always during dinner. You could always hang up the phone but this face-to-face stuff was more complicated.

Exhausted from both rides--the bike and my mind--I lay my head down on the pillow begging for sleep. I was looking forward to riding The Blue Ridge Parkway the next day.

CHAPTER 4
Virginia and the Luray Caverns

We started out the next day, heading for Skyline Drive, aka The Blue Ridge Parkway. Skyline Drive is a beautiful road but after 25 miles I was looking for a gun: no, not to shoot someone else, to shoot myself. Don't misunderstand me, I love riding the curves and seeing America in all its glory, but not behind thirty five foot trailers and mini vans driving at thirty five miles an hour.
"C'mon kids, there's the three hundredth lookout, let's stop and take a look again," I could hear the people in the cars in front of us: at least in my mind. It seemed interminable, but finally there was an exit. We got off Skyline Drive and shot over to Luray Caverns.

The caverns are really impressive, but if you are the least bit claustrophobic you have no shot to walk down the steps and into the caves, and there are points where you are more than one hundred feet below ground.
I wondered how the Maccabees, and other fighters in ancient Canaan felt, hiding in caves, battling overwhelming, powerful enemies. I would've called it Palestine, but it would give you the wrong impression as to how I feel.

> Sharon, Arafat and Bush were in a meeting
> negotiating what lands Israel was going to give
> back to the Palestinian people-the land that
> they claim to be rightly theirs. Arafat continuously
> claimed sovereign right. Sharon stood up and told
> this story:
> "Moses and Aaron were swimming in the Sea of
> Galilee on a very hot day. They'd shed their
> clothing and left them next to a rock a few feet from
> the water's edge. When they emerged from the
> Sea they saw that their clothing was gone.
> The people screamed to them: it was the
> Palestinians, the Palestinians stole your clothes!"
> Arafat jumped to his feet and shouted: "How can
> you say that, there were no Palestinians around at
> the time of Moses."
> "That's exactly the point," Sharon replied.
> "Now let's negotiate about giving back the land."

Actually there are a couple of funny Arafat stories.

> Arafat was feeling Ill so he went to a fortune-
> teller to see what was what.
> "You," the fortune teller said, "will die on a
> Jewish holiday."
> "Which Jewish holiday will that be?" Arafat
> queried.
> She replied: "any day you die will be a Jewish
> Holiday."

I always found it very curious, that my gentile friends could do anything on their holidays and we had to abide by, what seemed like, a zillion rules. They could drive places, go to ball games, watch T.V., play in the park, anything they wanted to do, while we were in Synagogue all morning, ate lunch with the family and either studied religious books or took a nap. Holy Day, which is where I thought the word came from would be much more appropriate. My friends would ask: "It's a holiday and you spend it in Synagogue? What kind of holiday is that?"

It's my belief that a group of people back in Jesus' day just wanted to 'reform' Judaism. It was very difficult to adhere to all of G-D's laws and they believed that the laws should be less stringent.

Judaism is the foundation of all western religions, and as such stands on its own. Christianity, on the other hand, can't stand alone; hell, it wouldn't exist without Judaism. Its entire foundation would be gone and the entire Christian world would be left hanging in mid-air with nothing holding it up.

We stopped at the bottom of the caverns and as I looked around at the stalagmites and stalactites, tons of questions continued racing through my mind: If the Ten Commandments were written by G-D and handed down to Moses, why does the Catholic bible have them in a different order than as originally written in the Old Testament (open any Pentateuch and, at the same time open up the Catholic version of the Old Testament and explain it to me)?

If G-D commanded us to "...remember the Sabbath...keep It holy," and the seventh day, the Sabbath was always on what we now call Saturday, then why do

Christians celebrate it on Sunday? Sabbath is supposed to be a day of rest, a day to recharge, so to speak. Yet Christians, for the most part, do whatever they please on their Sabbath.

So, what is the Sabbath, Shabbat as we call it in Hebrew, all about anyway? I tried to bring light to that question in a piece I wrote to my congregation.

Shabbes is the Yiddish and Shabbat the Hebrew. Even though Yiddish was the 'secret language' in my house, we always greeted each other in Yiddish: Gut Shabbes, Gut Yontif, Gut Voch, Gut Moid, Gut Yohr were the most common. Now I use mostly Hebrew: Shabbat Shalom, Shavua Tov, Chag Sameach, Moed Sameach and Shanah Tovah.

In my Shul when we say Havdalah we sing about having a good week. I sing shavua tov, the Hebrew, and the Rabbi sings a gutte voch, in counter point, in Yiddish. It's keeping the tradition that most of us who grew up in the 50s and 60s learned in our homes, the tradition that was sung in Ashkenazi Jewish homes for centuries and passed from generation to generation.

Shabbat, Shabbes, the Sabbath, the seventh day, it's the day that G-D rested after all his work creating the world; the day when G-D finally got the chance to exhale. Other than Yom Kippur, Shabbat is the holiest day of the year, and we get to celebrate her 52 times every year. We leave work early on Fridays so that we can prepare ourselves for Shabbat, so that we may be worthy of greeting the Sabbath Queen. The home is a sensory roller coaster, a cornucopia of aromas, tastes and sounds.

The women joyously preparing the Shabbat meal, a feast that even those who can ill afford it prepare, laugh in their kitchens as they knead the dough for the challah, make the fish and prepare the roast. The children, always in the kitchen, and always under-foot, are learning cooking secrets that have been handed down from bubby to bubby since, well, since who knows when. As the food cooks the home is permeated with olfactory delights.

The men go to the mikvah, purifying themselves in preparation of their greeting Shabbat HaMalka. And they dress! Oh yes, they dress in their best. Shabbat clothing is the finest clothing they own. They would never greet Shabbat in less than what they would wear to go and meet a member of royalty or the President of the United States, so to greet The King, The King of All Kings, The Holy One Blessed Be He, would you not wear your finest? Dresses, colorful and bright, hair done, faces scrubbed, the women await their husbands and fathers return from Shul.

And your dinner table would you not set that as for a 'feast fit for a king,' of course you would. The table is meticulously set with a beautiful, white tablecloth, white linen napkins and the finest silver, polished to a mirror finish.

Shabbat begins for the women when they light the candles. Heads covered, young girls standing at their sides, the women bring their hands over the flame, seemingly scooping the light, the warmth and the glow into their beings. The Shabbat candles burning, a particularly bright flame dancing on each candle top, greet the family as they gather around the table.

Lenny Mandel

The men say the Kiddush, everyone washes his hands (which is done by pouring water from an urn, onto one's hands, over a large bowl), says the 'motzi', eats a piece of the challah and sits.

The meal is a feast: gefilte fish, chopped liver, soup with mandlen, chicken or French roast, vegetables, dessert, oy, my mouth is watering right now.
They sit at the table singing; songs of Shabbat and songs of praise. It's warm, it's beautiful and it's safe.

On Shabbat the Shechinah, the Holy Presence, descends on the Earth, covering it. I feel safe even now just sitting here writing about it. That must be part of the answer about safety--you are surrounded by light, by family and by G-D, what could feel more secure than that?
This is a day of rest. No matter what day we choose to celebrate the Sabbath, it is time for our bodies to recharge, for our minds to relax. Don't we cram twenty five hours into every twenty four hour day? We run around for work, for ourselves for our families; G-D forbid we should have a day of rest.
See what it's like; c'mon take a deep breath. Good, now let it out—not so fast—let it out slowly! G-D took a long slow look at the work that He had done, and on Shabbat He exhaled. Shouldn't we?

The Church must have wanted to differentiate itself from Judaism as much as possible to make that change: hey, Shabbat is Shabbat. No? The rules are the rules, no? It's what I always thought.
Why don't Christians keep kosher? Aren't the first Five Books of The Bible, The Torah, The Pentateuch, the

ones that were actually written by G-D? Well, he commanded us, and that us is all inclusive, not to eat certain foods and yet Christians can eat whatever they want. That doesn't make sense according to G-D's commandments.

It's true that plenty of Jews do not follow the commandment of keeping kosher, but they made that a choice, a choice that they will pay for when they stand in front of the holy tribunal.

I made that choice as well and I remember the first time I went to a Chinese restaurant.

It was Philip Kinsler's ninth or tenth birthday and his parents took a bunch of us out. I don't remember if we went to the movies and then to eat, and I don't know how my parents allowed me to go with them if we were eating out, but I was there.

I have no recollection of anything that I ate, but I remember that they all had spare ribs and Elaine Kinsler told me that I couldn't eat them. The next course was a steaming hot, green thing all rolled up and a plate of this was put in front of each of us.

I turned to Elaine and whispered: "How do you eat this thing?" Elaine cracked up; it was a washcloth.

> *John and Morris, lifelong friends, decided to become ordained; John became a Roman Catholic Priest and Morris a Rabbi.*
> *Many years passed and on a stroll down Ocean Parkway John looked at Morris and said: "We've been friends for many years, Moish, and I know that it's against the tenets of your faith, against the law handed down to Moses, and*

against everything that you practice and believe in, but I have to ask you a question; have you ever tried pork?"
Morris, taken aback by the query, sat down on the nearest bench, stroked his beard while deep in thought and motioned for John to sit beside him.
"We've been friends a long time, John, and you are correct, it is against the tenets of my faith, against the law handed down to Moses, and against everything that I practice and believe in, but I'll answer you. Yes, I have tried pork."
John nodded, but before he could say anything, Morris raised his hand.
"John," he said, "you're right, we have been friends for many years, and I know that it's against the tenets of your faith and against everything that you practice and believe in, but I have to ask you a question; have you ever had sex?"
John stood up slowly, looked at Morris and said: "You are correct, it is against the tenets of my faith, and against everything that I practice and believe in, but I'll answer you. Yes, I have had sex."
Morris stood, put his arm around John's shoulder and said: "it's a lot better than pork!"

I don't remember the first time I ate food that wasn't kosher, but I'm sure it was that day.

There's a wonderful story about a Rabbi who was a huge Hemingway fan. He'd read every book, every essay and all the biographies written about him and he knew that Papa Hemingway's favorite restaurant was La Casa Botin in Madrid, Spain.

He also knew that Papa's favorite dish was roast-suckling pig, obviously a dish forbidden to him.
He traveled the footsteps Papa Hemingway took and found himself in Madrid; with great trepidation he entered Botin. He had to do it.
He had to try this dish although he knew the price he'd pay for it.
"Maybe," he thought, "if I do enough penance I'll be forgiven."
It was late in the evening, it was the middle of winter and, knowing that he wouldn't be seen by anyone he knew, he ordered the pig.
The waiter emerged from the kitchen carrying a large, covered silver tray, put it down in front of the Rabbi and took off the cover.
This was the most beautiful thing the Rabbi had ever seen, a delight to the eye from the tip of the pig's tail to the apple stuffed in its mouth.
He picked up his knife and fork and just as he was about to cut into the pig the president of his congregation walked in.
The Rabbi looked up and said: "you order a baked apple and look at the way it comes garnished!"

The Five Books of Moses set down laws and rituals to be followed and observed and the 'church' changed most of them so that people would accept Christianity as it wouldn't really change their lifestyles. I'm not looking for answers to these questions. They are, if nothing else, rhetorical and I don't need to hear Christian dogma or rhetoric about my musings. There is absolutely no doubt in my mind that Christian theologians have, over the past two thousand years, come up with fabulous answers to these unanswerable questions, So, for those of you who believe that you have the answers, keep them to yourselves; no doubt you've heard the questions before!

Understand this--I am not trying to negate, discount or belittle any faith; any path that brings you closer to 'The Big Guy' works for me. The problem is that most of you want to change us so that we follow your belief system, because yours is the 'true' faith, the only path; get over it and allow us to worship in our own way.

All of these interfaith squabbles, all this religious fanaticism makes me wonder about G-D's plan. Did He put us on this Earth (and that means everyone regardless of belief or lack thereof), and give us the freedom to make our own choices, our own mistakes, or is he The Grand Puppeteer? It's probably another argument that'll last forever.

> One of my favorite stories about our free will versus G-D's total control is about the farmer, who, while plowing his field hears a voice: "Sell your farm."
> He looks around but there's no one there. He continues and hears the voice again: "Sell your farm."
> Again he looks around but he's in the middle of a huge field and there is no one around.
> The next day he goes into town to buy supplies and he runs into his banker.
> "This is unbelievable," he says. "There I was, plowing my field and this voice told me to sell my farm."

The banker replied; "That really is unbelievable because I've got a guy in my office right now who wants to buy your farm."
The farmer makes the deal, walks out of the bank with a three and one half million dollar check, and hears the voice: "Go to Vegas."
He doesn't question.
He gets on the plane and goes, walks down the strip, walks into the casino at Caesar's Palace and he hears the voice: "Blackjack, play blackjack."
He sits down, pulls a hundred dollar bill from his pocket and he hears the voice: "Bet it all."
"Are you nuts," he screams.
"I said, bet it all," the voice adds.
The farmer puts the bank draft on the table, the pit boss ok's it, the cards are dealt and he draws a 19. He is about to stand pat when he hears the voice: "Take a card."
"Are you nuts," he screams, "I have a ..."
"I said take a card," the voice repeats.
He takes a card and draws an ace and hears the voice; "Take another card."
He takes another card, gets another ace, twenty-one, and he hears the voice "Unbelievable."

Yeah, it is pretty unbelievable that we are treated so differently by many Christians. It's as if we are not their ancestors.

Shakespeare was a huge anti-Semite and he even believed that Jews do everything everyone else does. Shylock's speech is so incredibly right-on that I can't believe Willie wrote it. Shylock is told that even if he doesn't get back the money owed him, he really wouldn't take the 'pound of flesh' anyway. What could it possibly be good for, Salerio queries?

"To bait fish withal..." Shylock answers. He wants revenge, if nothing more.

Shylock expounds on all the evil things done to him "...and what's his reason? I am a Jew."

These words send shivers up my spine and I recall all the crap I put up with just for being a Jew. Even now it sends a tear down my cheek, as I have asked these exact questions over and over through my wanderings and sufferings, benign though they are in the scheme of things, albeit not in MY scheme of things.

"Hath not a Jew eyes? Hath not a Jew hands, organs, dimensions, senses, affections passions? Fed with the same food, hurt with the same weapons, subject to the same diseases, healed by the same means, warmed and cooled by the same winter and summer as a Christian is?

If you prick us, do we not bleed? If you tickle us, do we not laugh? If you poison us, do we not die? And if you wrong us, shall we not revenge? If we are like you in the rest, we resemble you in that..."

I know all of this. I know that we are all created the same, right? We are, aren't we? Some bigger, some smaller, hairier, prettier, what's the difference--we all have something to give.

From Cross To Cross

All these thoughts were triggered by the fact that I was in a cave just as our ancestors were back in ancient times. We'd spent enough time below the surface and I'd spent more than enough time on the trip in my head. The four of us walked up the caverns and out into the sunlight while I, at the same time, surfaced from the recesses of my mind. It felt good to feel the sun's warmth on my skin and to shake the cobwebs' weavings out of my thoughts.

We mounted up, road south, and spent the night in Roanoke, Virginia. Little did I know that the next day's ride would be the impetus for all of these thoughts.

CHAPTER 5
Day Three the Back Roads of Virginia

Shelly's ear had an altercation with the pointy side of a hairbrush that night so, because of a visit to a local E.N.T. doc, we got a later start than anticipated. We rolled south down highway 221: one of the best motorcycle 'riding roads' I've ever traveled.

Sweeping curves going up the mountain just south of Roanoke made the beginning of the ride an absolute joy. Tight turns, almost switchbacks, changed immediately into wide sweeping curves as we rode up to the top, and unlike the Skyline Drive, we were able to crank up the speed. We liked it so much we both knew, albeit separately, that we'd stay on 221 all the way through North Carolina.

This road had Churches everywhere. Not Catholic Churches, Christian Churches, and of so many different denominations I couldn't figure out how one knew where to pray. It seemed to me that there was a Church on every corner, which would've been tough as there were very few 'corners' out here in rural Virginia for there to be Churches on.

Lenny Mandel

    Growing up, I never knew that churches other than Roman Catholic Churches existed. Protestants: What were they? Little did I know that one of the largest and most beautiful churches on Ocean Avenue, in Brooklyn, was an Episcopalian Church. As my friend Leila Dawson, who is an Episcopalian, told me: "it's like being Catholic without the guilt." Of course I knew that there were other religions, I just wasn't exposed to any but four: Jewish, Catholic, Moslem and Buddhist. I don't remember the details, but my mom took me to Chinatown and we went into a Buddhist Temple there; she always wanted to expose me to whatever there was so that I could learn.

    Virginia was rapidly passing under the wheels of our bikes and we stopped about fifteen miles from the North Carolina border to stretch our legs and down a quick drink. The four of us stood around checking out the map when I asked: "Where are all these Christians?" "C'mon," I asked again, "where are they? Where do these Churches get their congregants? Do they drive many miles as a part of a particular Christian denomination, to go to a specific Church?"

    The question was ingenuous; we were out in the sticks and there were dozens of Churches. At one point on route 221 there were three Churches, each a different denomination, within a hundred yards of each other.

    There were four or five Churches of The Brethren within three or four miles. What, they couldn't combine? Nobody lived anywhere in the area; they needed three Churches of the Brethren this close? I couldn't get over this.

There is the story of a man alone for eight years on a deserted island. A ship sees smoke billowing from the island and sends a boat to see what was up.
Upon landing the stranded man ran to the sailors, fell on his knees and thanked G-D for sending them to rescue him.
After feeding him the captain noticed that there were two buildings erected. He asked what the first building was.
"Ah," said the man, "that's the synagogue I belong to."
The captain asked: "Well then, what's the other building?"
"That," the man replied," is the synagogue I used to belong to."

Maybe, I thought, that's the story with all the Churches: naah, that's not what I thought.

I began to feel smaller and smaller. Not frightened, not scared, not apprehensive, not paranoid, I just felt small. My whole life I heard nothing but the great things Jews did, the myriad contributions they made to society in every walk of life. Hell, even Mark Twain wrote about it for Harpers in 1899:

If the statistics are right, the Jews constitute but one percent of the human race. It suggests a nebulous dim puff of the stardust lost in the blaze of the Milky Way. Properly, the Jew ought hardly be heard of but he is heard of, has always been heard of.

Lenny Mandel

He is as prominent on the planet as other people, and his commercial importance is extravagantly out of proportion to the smallness of his bulk.

His contributions to the world's list of great names in literature, science, art, music, finance, medicine, and abstract learning are also way out of proportion to the weakness of his numbers.

He had made a marvelous fight in this world in all the ages and has done it with his hands tied behind him. He could be vain of himself and be excused for it.

The Egyptians, the Babylonians, the Persians rose, filled the planet with sound and splendor, then faded to dream-stuff and passed away; the Greek and Roman followed, and made a vast noise, and they are gone; other people have sprung up and held their torch high for a time, but it burned out and they sit in twilight now, or have vanished.

The Jew survived all, beat them all, and is now what he always was, exhibiting no decadence, no infirmities of age, no weakening of his parts, no slowing of his energies, no dulling of his alert and aggressive mind.

All things are mortal but the Jew; all other forces, pass, but he remains.

What is the secret of this immortality?
Mark Twain, 1899.

When asked why I thought Jews were intellectually superior, or why I thought they made all these fantastic contributions to society, I always answer: "almost six thousand years of inbreeding."

Aside from being G-D's chosen people we were special, at least that's what we were taught to believe. So why then was I feeling so small, so insignificant? I was out of my element, and it seemed again as if I were a stranger in a strange land. How would these people take to me? What should I do, or how should I act, around them? Does my face scream: "I AM A JEW?"

It was back in 1970, when the headline and lead article of the newspaper in the Spanish city of Melilla--a tiny sliver of Spain that sits on the vast Northern coastline of Morocco--dealt with a huge drug ring that was busted the night before. It lauded the police on their prowess, having captured this cartel before they began exporting hundreds of kilograms of hash-hish out of Morocco, through Melilla and into the United States. The newspaper article was all bullshit, of course.

They caught five men and one woman who brought back half a kilo, or so, of keefe over a deserted border between Morocco and Spanish North Africa for their personal consumption. Truth be told, the man who sold them the keefe turned them in, got his drugs back, kept the money that they paid him and got a reward to boot. How do I know this? I was one of the six.

Our names were prominently printed in the newspaper: Mandel, Cohen, Holiner, Miller, Wagner and Peterson: with the exception of Wagner and Peterson, a veritable banquet of Jewish names. Wagner was Jewish as well but Peterson, my girlfriend, was Christian and a citizen of Denmark. One day a group of people visited us in prison. To say that we were surprised would be an understatement as the only people who knew we were even in prison were those from the American embassy, and they made it crystal clear that we deserved whatever fate the Spanish authorities had in store for us.

We walked into the visitor's area and were greeted by people from the Jewish community in Melilla; they'd read our names in the newspaper and wanted to know if we needed anything. They brought bread, cakes, fruit and lots of cigarettes for us. I raised my hands to the heavens, with palms facing inward and fingers outstretched; they looked at each other and said: "Ashkenazim."

They recognized this gesture as one used by a Jew whose heritage is from Eastern Europe; they were Sephardim. Sephardic Jews' ancestry is from Morocco, Spain, Greece, Turkey and the Middle East, and their rites and customs are very different from the Ashkenazim (another discussion for another time).

So, here I am, 3000 miles from New York City and am recognized, not only as a Jew, but as a Jew with Eastern European lineage, and I wonder if people know what I am just by looking at me?

I get the biggest chuckle when people wish me a Merry Christmas and then stop themselves and say: "I'm sorry, I mean have a happy Holiday."
"What?" I answer, "you don't want me to have a Merry Christmas too?"

So I ask myself again--do people know that I'm Jewish just by looking at me?

A wonderful parallel has to do with the movie, Dirty Dancing. A major film about the Catskills--the Jewish resort area about an hour and a half north of New York City also known as 'The Borsht Belt'--that starred Patrick Swayze and Jennifer Gray, and although filmed in Virginia, the setting looked as authentic as, well, as any hotel in the Catskills.

From Cross To Cross

    The film needed extras for background and scene work so they sent out letters to the local towns and filled three buses with extras. The buses arrived and all the extras had blonde hair, blue eyes and turned-up noses.
    The director was incensed. These people didn't look Jewish and would never do in the film. He sent his people back to the city to go to every Synagogue and Jewish Community Center to bring back Jewish extras. Two days later the buses returned carrying all the Jewish extras they could gather and every one of them had blonde hair, blue eyes and turned-up noses. It was a stitch.

    It was the same for Buddy Hackett when he finally agreed to go to Vermont and ski with his wife. She introduced him to the instructors.
    "I am Klaus, I am the commandant--no, no the head instructor…" The diatribe goes on but Buddy says that each of the ski instructors was six feet five inches tall, with fifty inch chests and thirty two inch waists, blonde hair, blue eyes, high cheekbones, turned up noses and gorgs (Adam's apples).
"Freaks," he said, "they were all freaks."
    It's not that there aren't Jews who look like that but the stereotypes are quite the opposite. On my mother's side of the family for example we are, for the most part, blonde haired and blue eyed. Of the seven first cousins there were five of us just like that--without the noses, cheekbones and gorgs of course.

    I guess I feel that people know that I'm a Jew just by looking at me and that's one of the things that bothers me. Not that I am a Jew but that I think that it's dangerous that I can be identified as one so readily.

We continued our ride down 221, with its rolling hills and sweeping turns. The sound of our wheels whirring across the pavement, always with us, continued as we crossed over the Virginia border into North Carolina. We stopped in Jefferson to grab a bite to eat.

Hardee's is not one of our usual spots, but it was time to grab a bite and, as I wasn't really eating anyway, I didn't care. You see, I'd started a diet the week before to lose a bunch of weight before our son's wedding in late August. Actually, it's a fast, a 500-calorie, five grams of fat a day diet. I eat (I should say drink) a 104-calorie packet of nutrients and protein, five times a day. Although I decided that I'd eat dinners on the ride, and make lunch an occasional treat, Hardee's wasn't exactly the treat I had in mind.

Chapter 6
The Same Day North Carolina

"May I have a jumbo diet cola and a half-cup of hot water please?" I asked.

The giggling on the other side of the counter spread to all the workers.

"Don't any Yankees stop here to eat? It's a favorite meal of theirs and I just wanted to see if it tastes the same South of the Mason-Dixon Line?"

The girls working there laughed although I'm sure they didn't get it.

While the four of us waited for our food, Hardee's started to fill up some (the flavor of the Southern way of speech has begun to permeate my writing), and everyone walked by our table to check the 'Yankees' out.

"How many people live in this town?" I asked the girl who took our order. She shrugged her shoulders and repeated my question to another girl sweeping at a nearby table.

"Dunno either," she replied. "I live about 35 minutes away from here," she said, "in a town called ..." It didn't matter because the town she lived in wasn't on the map of North Carolina. Trust me, we scoured our map with her standing right there pointing to where it should be even though it wasn't. She laughed as she pointed to a town 'right close.'

Lenny Mandel

There was a picture of the local High School football team on the wall, and one above it of the cheerleaders. These pictures were a sea of white faces and one black face. I was surprised that it was such a large team for such a small town; the High School, they let me know, was regional.

Three older men came in and sat together on one side of a booth. They positioned themselves so that they could see our bikes and hear us. I didn't want to ask about the black kid on the team as the old Grand Wizard and his two aging henchmen were paying rapt attention to our conversation; KKK, I thought.

Pictures of Jack Nicholson getting beaten to death in Easy Rider ran through my mind and I spat so that it wouldn't come true; I thought about what I'd just done and laughed out loud as the words from the song Eve of Destruction ran through my mind: "…hate your next door neighbor, but don't forget to say Grace…"

The sky was becoming darker, the black clouds were getting lower and lower, so we ran out to the bikes, grabbed our rain-gear and waited for the deluge; three minutes later it came.

Nobody was leaving Hardee's without Noah's ark for safe passage, so a few people came over to hang out with us and talk. An older man there rode a Gold Wing as well and regaled us with stories of some of his trips, one to Alaska.

Alaska was a trip that my buddy Wulf Sonne and I planned to take a few years back until a bunch of guys from our H.O.G. chapter decided to join us. It's not that I would've minded riding with these guys, but two motorcyclists have enough potential problems on a ride, most of which would be solved quickly. Throw in a third bike, these problems grow, and with the fourth and the fifth bike they grow exponentially.

We all sat down one night and started making plans.

"Lenny, you'll carry the tent behind you," someone said. "Tent?" I said, "you've gotta be kidding! This (pointing to myself) is a Jewish person. My idea of roughing it is when room service is ten minutes late!"

After the laughter subsided I said, "The tent will be good support for my back on a long ride like this so here's what I'll do. I'll help you pitch the tent, start the fire and come back to eat with you after I've checked in at the nearest motel. There has to be a motel within a ten-minute radius, and in the morning I'll be back for breakfast and to help you break camp." Needless to say the trip never happened.

I found out, after the fact, that one of the guys who wanted to come with us sold Swastikas and other hate paraphernalia at his booth at biker rallies. It would have made for some interesting discussion around our campfire in the backwoods of Canada, don't you think?

CHAPTER 7
Swastikas throughout my life

These stories deviate from this ride, but not from the ride I took my whole life, neither from the ride my mind traveled riding these back roads.

    I think about all the 'bikers' sporting all of that hate shit and it really pisses me off. Aside from the fact that I'm an old time-left wing-Jewish liberal who marched in Washington, was a member of the New York Sane Society, a 'peacenik' and all that goes with it was irrelevant. I hate, hate, I mean I really hate it. It angers me and scares me at the same time. What myth do these guys think they are perpetuating? True, some of them are truly scary characters--people to be feared--but some are accountants who go back to work on Monday after riding their Harleys fifty miles with the boys on Sunday.

    I truly understand why the early 1%ers wore swastikas. It wasn't to show anyone that they were anti-establishment, it wasn't a 'screw you,' the swastikas they wore were trophies.
    The first motorcycle gang, the outlaw bikers as it were, were a group of disgruntled World War II veterans who felt totally out of sync with mainstream society. They wore denim vests with the name of their gang boldly

displayed on its back, and the plethora of patches on the front of their vests stood for myriad things.

There might've been a '13' or an 'M' which stood for marijuana, a '1%' patch which means that 1% of all people who ride motorcycles are outlaws or a big '1' which means the same. There are many patches worn by bikers today and most of them are laughable; the one that isn't is the swastika.

    Don't think for a moment that I believe that those men, the soldiers back from WWII, were Nazis or Nazi sympathizers: not at all. They were American soldiers home from abroad, many of them heroes. They were the victors of a horrible war, and we all know that "...to the victors belong the spoils."

    The swastikas and the iron crosses that they displayed proudly on their chests were just that: spoils of war, trophies, and medals that they themselves ripped from the uniforms of their defeated foes. Even the German helmets that they wore when riding were trophies. They didn't have to wear them; there were no helmet laws back then.

    None of these trophies was any different from the scalps that the Indians shaved off of their enemies' heads and displayed proudly on their belts. These were badges of courage and of honor. They spoke silent volumes of the deeds of these warriors who rode into battle, stood face to face with the enemy and won. They were their Silver Star, their Navy Cross, and their Medal of Honor.

    Well it's not the 1940s, and those 'trophies' from WW II, the swastika, the iron cross and the German army helmets are still vivid reminders of an horrific time. They remind us of an era where insanity reigned and where murder, torture and greed were the credo. It was a time when a megalomaniac, who fanned the flames of hate until that hate ravaged everything in its path, used the swastika as his symbol. The swastika adorned every Nazi flag and the uniform of every soldier. It was raised high in the air on the banners that led the armies as they marched, and was even worn as an armband by young children.

The 1%er's have always worn them and still do, but it's no longer a badge of honor, nor is it a trophy. No, now it is a 'screw you'. It's a way of showing the world that they don't care about anything, and it's as subtle as a brick thrown through a plate glass window. So what the hell is the non 1%er doing wearing a swastika? Does he think it's cool, that he looks tough, that it instills fear in people, or is he just stupid?

A bunch of guys from my H.O.G. chapter were at Americade a few years ago when I had a problem with my bike that needed more skill to fix than I possessed. There was a kid, nineteen or twenty years old, hanging out at the motorcycle shop and he sported a swastika on his 'brain-bucket.' When I asked him why it was there he told me that he thought it was 'cool.' Cool, wow! He had absolutely no understanding of what the swastika stood for, and we had a half of an hour conversation so that he could be enlightened.

For those of you who don't live on the East Coast, Americade takes place in Lake George, N.Y., which is a gorgeous resort town in the Adirondack Mountains about three and a half hours north of N.Y.C. We're not talking about the deep South where the Klan has many minions, the Klan in this area hasn't a bang; actually up there one can hardly hear a whimper. Yet there are vendors at this rally, and most other rallies as well, selling hate. These vendors aren't sanctioned by or even part of, the event, but set up shop on the outlying fringes of the rallies anyway. The problem is that plenty of bikers buy the crap that these people sell.

At one of these fringe vendor areas we walked into a booth where, among the helmet stickers that he was selling were swastikas. I asked him why and he said, "Hey, it's America." Yes, he is right, it is America, and he was free to sell swastikas, and I was free to walk away--which I did.

Not only was he a member of my H.O.G. chapter, he was also a part owner in the restaurant where we met. I inquired about having the meetings elsewhere. The director of the chapter told me to "stop grandstanding ...the members of the chapter were there to have fun, and if you bring up this swastika stuff..." Needless to say I never set foot in that restaurant again.
That member wanted to go to Alaska with us--no shot!

There are many beautiful bikes up at Americade and a favorite pastime is to stand and watch them as they pass. One beautiful Harley Heritage, sporting a brand new paint job, stopped at a light. Both the rider and his passenger were wearing brand new leathers, his gold Rolex peeking out of the sleeve of his jacket, and the German helmet that didn't quite cover his longish gray hair had a swastika on it.

Why in G-D's name was he wearing a swastika? Why would any reasonably intelligent, rational person wear a swastika in this day and age? Hmmm, reasonably intelligent, yes, that's the key.

This is the guy you've gotta grab by the lapels (or the balls if you dare). This wasn't the young kid at the shop. This was a forty plus year old who knew what the swastika was and who was only one generation away from serving in WWII, fighting against everything that it stood for.

The problem is that he isn't alone; there are plenty of bikers still wearing swastikas and they all have to be made to understand that the swastika isn't a trophy anymore.

The people at Kuryakin hired a technician who brazenly wore a short sleeve shirt so that the swastika--tattooed on his forearm--was in plain sight.
What am I missing?

Do I sound pissed off? I hope so, because I am! I'm tired of hearing racial and ethnic slurs and seeing banners of hate. I'm tired of the apathy and I'm tired of watching so many of you turn away as if it doesn't exist or isn't there. Here's how I feel about it: if they can stand up displaying their symbols of hatred and bigotry unabashedly, why the hell are you still sitting?

In 1985 my house was the target of what I thought was a 'mischief night' prank. Mischief night is the night before Halloween and in many neighborhoods there are kids who cover the trees with toilet paper, throw eggs, scatter garbage and other annoying but not harmful or hateful things. Despite the negligible nature of these acts we always left the outside lights on all around the house on Mischief night.

Lenny Mandel

My family and I drove up the block that evening to grab a bite to eat and pick up a leather coat that Shelly had ordered. There were a dozen or so kids hanging out at the top of our street, and I thought about turning around and getting the coat the next day but didn't. The trees on the block next to ours were festooned with toilet paper when we returned, and I smiled, albeit with tongue in cheek, wondering what our street would look like. There was plenty of toilet paper there as well and as we drove down the street and approached our house I saw what looked like smearing on the windows.

"It was our turn," I thought, and it would have been the first time our house had been egged in the ten years that we lived here.

Throwing raw eggs at a house was a major mischief night prank as eggs stuck and were a real pain to wipe off after they dried. All six of the front windows were hit and both front doors, but as I got closer I saw that the white markings dripping down the windows and doors were not eggs: they were swastikas spray painted onto each surface. I was burning mad but my family was terrified.

As I walked around the back of the house, there was a swastika painted on my deck and, in letters three feet high on the sliding glass doors that led from our kitchen onto our deck, the word JEW. I called the police but before they arrived I grabbed a baseball bat and headed up the street. My neighbors were already out and, for the most part they were armed as well. I knocked on every door asking the kids if they heard or saw anything but they all said no. Most of them lied and most of them were Jewish.

From Cross To Cross

One can of spray paint was tossed into a sewer up the block and I rang the bell at the house and questioned the oldest sibling: he was sixteen. I knew he was lying by the way he averted his eyes when he answered me. I told him that he'd tell the truth to the police when they pulled him out of class when he was at school the next day.

His mom was pretty upset with me but I didn't care, I was seething. I walked out of his house and his mom asked me to come back; I did and he told me the truth.

To this day I hear my son crying himself to sleep that night, wondering when 'they' were going to come back and get us, and I hear myself praying that my parents wouldn't decide to take a drive out to visit us and see the horrors that they had fled forty six years earlier. I thanked G-D that I hadn't caught them in the act or after the fact as I would have been arrested and thrown in jail for, at least, assault with a deadly weapon.

The details aren't important anymore nor are the names of the kids who painted my house. Yes, the kids, neither of whom was Jewish, were caught (I knew who they were thirty minutes after I was home) and one of the parents came over to our house. He was completely embarrassed and at a loss for words. The other boy's mother called crying hysterically on the phone. She couldn't understand how her son who did so many good, charitable things could do such a thing. I tried to console her but Shelly wouldn't hear of it; "fuck them," she screamed.

"Fuck them, let them go to jail, let them suffer as we're suffering:" these words from a woman, my wife, who doesn't curse.

Lenny Mandel

So after living a vicarious hell through the eyes of my parents and their peers, we too felt the whips of hatred flaying our skin and burning our own eyes.
The swastika: may those who wear it and believe in it suffer a painful, tortuous death.

Looking out the window from our table in Hardee's we could see that this North Carolina storm wasn't going to go away, so we donned our rain suits, walked past the stares of the three old-timers, waved goodbye to our new friends and left.

It wasn't raining terribly hard as we left Hardee's and 221 opened up into a four lane highway. That's when the sky opened up, just as we hit that highway. I don't mean that the sun broke through; I mean it started to pour, the wind kicked up, and I couldn't see five feet in front of my bike. I slowed down hoping it would make it easier--no such luck.

They're getting me, I thought. It's a forced baptism. Could they actually do that to me? I laughed out loud.

It's the story of the man who, drunk, and stumbling through the woods comes upon a preacher baptizing people in the river.
He walks into the water and bumps into the preacher who asks: "Are you ready to find Jesus?"
The drunk answers," Yes, I am."
With that the preacher grabs him and dunks him. He pulls him up and asks: "Brother, have you found Jesus?"
No, I haven't," the drunk replies.

Shocked, the preacher dunks him again, this time longer.
He pulls him out and repeats the question,
"Have you found Jesus, my brother?"
Again the drunk answers no.
At his wits end, the Preacher throws the drunk down into the water, holding him there until his arms and legs are flailing.
The preacher asks: "tell me, please for the love of G-D tell me that you've found Jesus?"
The drunk, spitting water from his mouth while trying to dry his eyes, catches his breath and says "Are you sure this is where he fell in?"

It rained and rained and rained some more. Tropical storm Bill's leading edge, no doubt. Where was Noah's ark when we needed it?

When the waters overran the Mississippi a few years ago there were floods that wiped out entire communities. A Rabbi was standing in front of his Synagogue, water up to his waist when a rowboat pulled up.
"C'mon Rabbi, get in," the man in the boat hollered.
"No," the Rabbi replied, "I have been a devout Jew my entire life. G-D will save me."
About three hours later, the Rabbi was still standing in front of his Synagogue, with the water now up to his shoulders.
"Rabbi, get in, get in the boat" the man in the boat hollered again.

> "No," the Rabbi again replied, "I have been a devout Jew my entire life. G-D will save me."
> Another three hours passed, the water covered the entire Synagogue, and the Rabbi drowned.
> The Rabbi stood in front of the Holy Tribunal, faced G-D and said, "I have been a devout Jew my entire life G-D, I followed every commandment, why didn't You save me."
> G-D sat, looked straight at the Rabbi and said: "Shmuck, I sent the rowboat twice!"

Although everybody wants to ride in the sunshine, Shelly is a real trooper, and knows what it means to get caught in the rain. The first couple of years that I had my 'big' bike she only took short rides with me, but since 1993 we've taken long trips every year. It helps that the new bike (I forsook Harley for a 2002 Honda Gold-Wing last year) is unbelievably comfortable and has a six CD changer in the trunk--yup, it's got a trunk.

We take forty or fifty CDs with us and she humors me by 'allowing' me to listen to The Allman Brothers, The Grateful Dead or some of my more esoteric music along with her choices. I usually change the CDs every morning and I throw in a couple that I know she won't love but at seventy five miles an hour what's she gonna do, jump off?

The only CD she really hates is by Tom Waites. I love it but she might actually jump if she had to listen to him for forty five minutes--believe me Tom, you're on my changer whenever she isn't on the bike.

I know that you're going to re-read the piece where you just read that I ride a 'wing' now. Don't bother; it's true. I sold my '89 FLHS and bought a new Harley Ultra in

From Cross To Cross

2002. I hated it. I was on the phone to Harley Davidson twice a week, to no avail. Here's the letter I sent them regarding their bike.

"In May of this year I bought a new (2002) Ultra from Liberty Harley in Rahway, New Jersey (I've been going there since they opened, their 'lead tech' is a very close friend of mine, and I've never had a problem with them). After a couple of days of riding I called to complain about the heat emanating from the engine and was told: "You'll get used to it."

That wasn't a good enough answer for me but they said that it would probably subside after 'break-in'; it didn't. I called Harley (Milwaukee) many times and got the same 'no-answer'. I removed the lowers but still the heat was unbearable.

In the two and one half months that we've owned this bike we've put on about 4700 miles, but I have never hated a motorcycle, in all my thirty seven years of riding, until now.

We pulled off the highway in the Green Mountains of Vermont and my legs were scalded. We rode into N.Y.C. for dinner one evening and, because we had to sit in the Holland Tunnel for five minutes, the heat was so intense that my wife couldn't bear it. It actually burned her legs.

This exquisitely beautiful machine is being sold as I write this letter and I, who have ridden nothing but Harley, BSA, Triumph or Norton since 1969 (when I got my first HD--a 1946 flathead with a tank shift and suicide clutch) am contemplating buying a Honda Gold Wing. I sold an FLHS that I bought brand new in 1989 so that I could buy this bike. The FL was a one hundred four cubic inch stroker and we rode her for more than sixty five thousand miles. My wife, who has been riding with me (two up) for 16 years wanted more comfort, a radio, etc so where else would I go? I bought the Ultra.

Don't think that the '89 FL was my only bike. Since 1989 I also owned a: '74 sporty, an '89 tricked out springer, a '94 FXDWG, a '70 Triumph Bonneville chopper and a 1951 Panhead chopper.

I am amazed that you would market a bike like the Ultra; more so when the techs at HD in Milwaukee told me that they had myriad complaints about the heat it throws off. Has your own mystique rubbed off on your engineering staff to the point that you just don't care?

I must tell you that of the three major touring bikes, the Wing, the BMW K1200LT and the Ultra, yours is certainly the most beautiful and that's it. Out of those three bikes the Ultra comes in a distant ninth.

My '89 FL didn't emit ten percent of the heat that this new ultra does and the rhetoric about the engine being larger and there being one third more surface area doesn't mean much when you have to put up with that kind of heat.

My wife and I were in Naples, Florida this past April when we rented a 2002 Road King. In the heat of Florida, in four miles of bumper to bumper traffic going to Sanibel Island, and riding at ninety five mph through Alligator Alley we didn't feel anywhere near this kind of heat. We loved the bike, and it was this ride that forced me to buy the Ultra. I got off the bike and told the dealer that it had been the most expensive ride of my life.

He, visibly shaken, began walking around the bike looking for signs of damage.

"No, no," I said, "this is gonna cost me twenty three grand for a new Ultra."

It's been a while since I began this letter and since then I bought a new Honda Gold-Wing, and it is fabulous. It is quicker, faster, smoother, better engineered, better finished and handles a zillion times better than the Ultra ever could—even in the dreams of your engineers the Ultra couldn't come up to snuff against the wing, and in the three weeks since I bought it my odometer reads twenty six hundred fifty miles.

If your concept of selling motorcycles is to cater to the crowd that is only interested in 'garage-candy', I think that you are doing very well.
It's time you looked at those of us who are 'bikers' yet part of the mainstream, and manufactured a product both beautiful and utile.
I've never pictured myself without a Harley in my garage, but the reality is that the three bikes I now own are a Wing, a BMW K1200RS and a sport bike for back-roads and the track.
Thank you for your ears (or in this case, eyes-- actually I have a chopper in my garage as well)."

The smell of fresh cut grass brought me back to the moment at hand, riding down route 221. That aroma is one of my favorites and it was that smell, interspersed with honeysuckle and jasmine that enticed my olfactory senses along 221. I always associated the sweet smell of freshly cut grass with my summers in the 50s, away from the city, when I was in camp. That's where I met my Canadian pal Bobby some fifty years earlier.

CHAPTER 8
Prelude to The Rides

I first met Bobby Lash at Camp Bayview in 1953. The camp was nestled in Quebec's Laurentian Mountains, on Lac Archambault, right outside the village of St. Donat. Bobby and I became buddies from day one, and we remained such for all the years he went to camp. This wasn't as easy as it sounds--Bobby lived in Montreal and I in New York.

Almost all of the campers were Jewish and I never even thought of the problems regarding the French-Canadians and anti-Semitism; I was told that we weren't allowed at Gray Rocks or Mont Tremblant, two major ski resorts in the Laurentians. I knew about the racism in Miami, Florida so I didn't find it odd. Racism was just another part of my life that I'd have to learn to deal with.

Arthur Godfrey had a hotel (in Miami or Miami Beach) that had a sign on the front lawn that read: "No Jews, No Dogs, No Niggers;" It's why I spit every time I go over the Arthur Godfrey Causeway.

My father used to tell the story of a man that went down to the Kenilworth Hotel in Florida to spend the winter.

This man walks up to the front desk and says in a very heavy Eastern European accent: "Hallo, I have a reservation here for the winter."
The manager says: "you must be mistaken, didn't you see the sign, we don't allow Jews in this hotel."
I'm not a Jew," he replied," I'm a Catholic."
"A Catholic?" he queried, "with that accent? Prove it to me. What's the name of our Lord?"
"Jesus," the man answers.
And what were his parent's names?"
"Mary and Joseph," he replied.
"And where was Jesus born?"
"In Bethlehem," he replied.
"And exactly where in Bethlehem was he born?"
"In a stable," he replied.
"And why was he born in a stable?"
The man looked the manager in the eye and said: "because an anti-Semitic hotel manager like you wouldn't let his mother in."

Actually I had a situation just like that happen to me when I was competing in trap-shooting.

The envelope, with The New York Athletic Club name and logo in the upper left hand corner, was addressed to Leonard J. Mondale, at my address. The NYAC's location up at Travers Island, was holding it's annual trap-shooting contest, and as a member of the A.T.A. (the amateur trapshooting association) I was invited.

I laughed when I saw the way my name was misspelled, but I had never been allowed to compete at any NYAC event, hell, I wasn't allowed inside the doors, it was a restricted club. I decided to go.

I told Fred Remington, not only a shooting buddy of mine but a state assemblyman (or something to that effect), that I was going to Travers Island. He looked at me and said: "How the hell did you get invited?"

"They misspelled my last name," I told him, "but I'm going anyway."

He laughed and asked me what time I was going to check in. He wanted to be there to see the look on their faces when I told them my real name.

I loaded my car with a case of shells, two different shooting vests, earplugs, shooting glasses and, of course, my invitation and directions to Travers island. I cleaned my shotgun, left it next to my bed and went to sleep.

I smiled the whole drive there and as I walked over to the sign-in table I spotted Fred who gave me a big hello.
"Name please," the man at the desk asked.
"Lenny Mandel," I replied.
"We don't have anyone with that name registered," he said.
"Ah, yes," I said, "that's because you misspelled my name on the invitation; here it is."
"There must be some mistake," he said.

The phone rang on the army base in Alabama, and a woman in a deep southern drawl spoke:
"Captain, I know that some of our boys won't be able to go home for Thanksgiving, so I'm extending an invitation to a couple of them to join me for Thanksgiving dinner at my home.

*One thing though, captain, I'd prefer you
don't send anyone of the Jewish persuasion."
The captain agreed and on Thanksgiving day the
two soldiers knocked on the woman's door.
She came to the door and standing on her porch
were two of the biggest black men she'd ever seen:
each was 6'5" tall and, easily. 265 lbs.
"There m-m-must be some mistake," she
stammered.
"No ma'am,"they replied, "Captain Goldberg don't
make no mistakes."*

"I don't think that there is a mistake, the numbers match, you just misspelled my name," I reiterated, leaning over the table with the Magen David around my neck dangling in his face.

Fred Remington, who was standing there grinning, jumped in: "His invitation is legit. Let him shoot." They did although there were mistakes made in scoring and I turned around once with a loaded shotgun in my hand and asked for the director.

Needless to say I didn't fare very well, the distractions were far too, well, distracting, but the point was made and that's all I cared about. You can bet that I wasn't invited the following year. The Mandel accompanied by my Star of David sealed my fate.

So how, after so many years, did I finally hook up with Bobby again? It's one helluva story.

In 2001 my wife Shelly and I took a motorcycle trip up to Canada. Originally we were headed for Prince Edward Island, one of the Maritime Provinces in Canada, for the Canadian National H.O.G. rally. It was a trip that I had talked about for a long time and this was going to be the year.

We'd already ridden to Nova Scotia twice, with my friend Sonne in '96 and with Shelly in '99. That's when our trips to Canada began. The ride in '96 was supposed to be a couple of days to 'clear the cobwebs'—it was.

Chapter 9
Nova Scotia 1996

My trip with Sonne in 1996 and my trip with Shelly in 1999 began exactly the same way. We rode out of New Jersey, through New York State, and into Connecticut. My helmet was off as soon as we passed the 'Welcome to Connecticut' sign. I put my helmet back on in Massachusetts took it off again and stowed it for the rest of the trip in The United States: New Hampshire and Maine.

    The Scotia Prince is a ship, which sails nightly to Yarmouth, Nova Scotia, from Portland, Maine, its belly filled with two wheelers, four wheelers of every description and eighteen wheelers as well. We figured that we'd have to spend the night in a motel anyway, so why not sleep on an overnight ferry and wake up in Canada. It was, as they say, a plan.
    As Sonne and I waited to board the ship in 1996, U.S. Custom's agents walked up to the bikes.
    "Proof of citizenship, please," the agent asked me. I handed him an old passport of mine. He took the passport, walked over to the fence and started talking on his two-way radio.
    "Are you carrying any drugs," asked the second agent?

"Yes", I said, "Prilosec for my esophagus."

"I mean any illegal drugs, you know what I'm talking about," he said.

"No", I said, "we figured that if we wanted any dope we could buy it in Canada." Sonne and I thought that was pretty funny--we were the only ones (funnier still, neither one of us smokes dope).

It didn't take them long to go through my saddlebags, Lucas bag and belly bag, and of course, there was nothing for them to find. Ironically, of all the bikes there, the only ones they picked to check were ours; as the customs agents put it, "you guys don't look like stockbrokers."

We were wearing black leather jackets, leather berets, jeans and boots, and my hair, which is pretty long, must've looked like a bird's nest after having ridden the last couple of hours without a helmet. Ok, so they were wrong--maybe they don't know what stock brokers really look like.

Riding my bike onto the ferry made me feel a kinship with Jonah: you know who I mean, the guy in the whale. There is this gaping, mouth like hole and it swallows you up as you ride in. Given the fact that motorcycles are first off, you're directed to the end of the hold, through the bottom of this whale's belly near the end of the large intestine.

We cleared customs again, in Canada, of course, and now it was time to ride.

We rode out onto Highway 103/3 heading for Halifax, the capital of Nova Scotia, but we wanted to ride the coast, so, we made a right turn toward the stronger smell of salt in the air.

From Cross To Cross

    The Nova Scotia coastline is gorgeous. The rock formations, fishing boats, churches and homes are what the great seascape artists must have relied on for their work.
    It was a slow but wonderful ride and, to my amazement, I couldn't get enough of it. We rode a few hours, were hungry, a little tired and so we stopped in Lunenburg.
    We found a restaurant in this quaint town on the coast. It overlooked a pier on which a folk festival was being held. The local beer was wonderful, the music reminiscent of my days as a folk singer in the 60s, and the fresh fried clams were scrumptious. We sat there for more than an hour just drinking in the beauty of the place and marveling over our good fortune. The fact that the exchange rate was incredibly in our favor didn't hurt either.
    After filling our bellies and resting our aching muscles, we headed out on the highway to Halifax. Unbeknownst to us we would be getting into Halifax right in the middle of the Busker's Festival. Okay, you're thinking, what's a busker?
    A busker is a street performer, and these buskers are there by invitation only. They come from all over the world, and the variety of acts and the talent that come is amazing.

    Sonne and I found a room almost immediately at a beautiful four-star hotel and, with the exchange rate being what it was, the room cost about sixty two dollars a night. Double beds, a hot shower, bathrobes and breakfast: it was more than we needed but certainly welcomed.

Lenny Mandel

That night we walked down to the pier, where we stood for a couple of hours watching jugglers, mimes, musicians and clowns. We listened to myriad musicians-- from solo acts to ten-piece Peruvian guitar bands--and watched unicyclists try not to land on their heads. None of these acts get paid; they work for tips, which they solicit by passing the hat.

There were face painters, along with vendors of tie dye T-shirts, and avant-garde jewelry. There were people selling knit goods from the Andes, hatters, caricaturists the list goes on and on. I was back in the 60s.

We'd spent two glorious days riding, and with neither of us getting much sleep on the ferry, we hit the pillows early (it doesn't take much to lull you to sleep in a four-star hotel).

Day three dawned, oh yeah, we saw the dawn (NOT). This was going to be a day to rock & roll down the highway, up through the center of Nova Scotia to the New Brunswick border and turn west along the Northern coast of The Bay of Fundy heading back to Maine. There is a tidal timetable for the Bay of Fundy as it is a huge tourist attraction. When the tide is out, all the boats lie on their sides on the sand (in essence the bottom of the bay). When the tide comes in, it does so as a wall of water and the boats pop up as if they were slices of bread out of a toaster. It's called the tidal bore. They say that it's a sight to see. Unfortunately we didn't see it.

There is a time difference in the Maritimes, and although we awoke in plenty of time to get to the tip of the Bay of Fundy and watch the tidal bore, our watches were an hour later than the local time. Go know!

From Cross To Cross

We flew along the coastline, setting our sights on Calais (pronounced callis), Maine where we would re-enter the good old USA. We decided to ride all the way down to Bar Harbor and spend the night. It was that evening that Sonne, while riding behind me as the sun was setting, took the picture, that I water-colored and used for the cover of this book.

We pulled into Bar Harbor five hundred fifty miles later on this glorious Saturday night in August and began looking for a place to stay. What karma, we found the only vacancy for twenty miles. If you've ever been to Bar Harbor, on a Saturday night in August you know it's the truth. We chained the bikes to each other, covered them up and went into the room. Trust me, this was as far from a four-star hotel as one could get.

We woke up to the screeching of seagulls; I went outside to check the bikes while Sonne went to wash up, and as I turned to go back into the room, there stood Sonne with the sink in his hands. It seems that while brushing his teeth he leaned on it to spit his toothpaste out and when he stood up the sink came with him. We laughed for five minutes, and after looking the Motel over we renamed it The Bates Motel (you do remember Psycho).

It's over five hundred miles from Bar Harbor to home, and that's where we were heading, home. We'd had enough coastline scenery, it was time to ride inland on the interstate (you've gotta love those highway pegs at 85 miles per hour). We booked most of the way home with the usual stops on the side of the highway, stopped at Sonne's house, gave each other a big hug, and said good bye.

Lenny Mandel

It was a great trip and one that I'd have to do again albeit differently; you need to spend at least six days in Nova Scotia to really experience the Province. The difference in the sights and terrain is incredible, and you really have to go in early August. You shouldn't miss those buskers.

I rode the remaining eleven miles to my house with a huge smile on my face. It seems like I do that all the time.

Well, Sonne backed out of our 2001 ride to the Canadian H.O.G. rally; he bought a new house, a 'fixer-upper', and was in the middle of a dozen projects. No problem, Shelly and I would go alone. There never seems to be a shortage of other bikers on the road, anyway, and less so if you're headed to a H.O.G. rally.

Prince Edward Island, let's see, we'll ride to Maine, stop a couple of times on the water to slurp down some 'fish' and spend the night in Bar Harbor. Boogie the next day through New Brunswick (no, not New Jersey) and head into P.E.I. From there, well, who knows?

CHAPTER 10
The 2001 Ride To Montreal

Since Shelly and I did a ride to Nova Scotia in 1999, and I couldn't come up with a really good reason for doing another Maritime ride, I started to look elsewhere for this ride in 2001.

Lancaster County, Pennsylvania sounded like a nice ride. Go to Gettysburg. See the battlegrounds of the Civil War. Spend some time in Amish country. Ride down to the Smokeys, or up to Cleveland to the Rock and Roll Hall of Fame (c'mon now, is there any other reason to go to Cleveland--just kidding--no, wait, doesn't John Rocker pitch for the Indians now? Maybe he's got some things to say about the folks there!); another time maybe, but not now. It seemed that I couldn't decide on a destination that excited me.

"What about Montreal," I thought. I'd spent eight to ten weeks a year for eleven summers in a camp about seventy five miles north of Montreal in the Laurentian Mountains, and a week or two every winter in Montreal. Forty years, hmmm, forty years since I'd been back. It was a done deal; we were going to go to Montreal.

We planned a seven-day trip. Montreal, up to the Laurentians, back roads through Southwestern Quebec to Ottawa, Toronto, Niagara Falls, upstate New York and

home. It was a bit optimistic for so short a trip but we decided to go for it. So at nine in the morning, Saturday June 30th, we packed the bike and headed north.
We decided to boogie up to Montreal, stopping as little as possible, so that we could spend most of our time riding in Canada.

It was a gorgeous day Saturday June 30, 2001; eighty-plus degrees, bright sunshine and, for a while, very little humidity. We rode onto the New York State Thruway, with huge smiles on both of our faces as the wheels rolled over the pavement, singing I'm on the road again by Canned Heat. A few minutes passed and we felt a raindrop and then another; what a way to start a trip. I've been riding for many years and although I ride in the rain, I don't love it.
I looked up at the sky and all I saw was blue. I'm still wondering where the drops came from because that was all the rain there was, so I smiled, set the thumbscrew and purred along. Actually my 'Thunder-Headers' don't purr, they growl, a low, throaty growl, but that's purring to me, no kitten sitting on my lap could sound sweeter (no pun intended--although knowing bikers like I do, I'm sure most of you have huge grins on your faces).

A three mile backup on the Thruway didn't help the ride but the exit sign, Bethel, New York, had me singing again.
    I came upon a child of God
    He was walking along the road
    and I asked him where are you going?
    And this he told me.

From Cross To Cross

I'm going on down to Yasgur's farm
I'm gonna join in a rock and roll band,
I'm gonna camp out on the land
and try and get my soul free.

Then can I walk beside you
I have come here to lose the smog.
And I feel to be a cog
in something turning.

Well maybe it is just the time of year,
or maybe it's the time of man,
And I don't know who I am
but you know life is for learning.

By the time we got to Woodstock
we were half a million strong,
and everywhere there was song and celebration.
And I dreamed I saw the bombers
riding shotgun in the sky,
And they were turning into butterflies
above our nation ...

**We are stardust, we are golden and we've got to get ourselves back to the garden

I sang the whole song, twice. It was a different world and I realized, at that moment, that our trip to Canada was going to take me back many, many years to a much simpler time.

Summer camp in the 50s was a time of folk singing, a time of swimming in the lake, of ingenuosity (or

is that ingenuousness?), of raising the flags each morning (both Canadian and American), of sing-downs, of childhood friendships that you swore would never end, of kick the can, and ring-a-leevio, of run-sheep-run, Johnny on the pony and hide and go seek. Socials and talent shows, canoe trips, bonfires, raids on the girl's side of the camp…hmmm I could go on and on and on.
We took a 40 minute pit stop at the top of the Thruway, were rejuvenated, mounted up and headed north.

    I've been to Americade many times but hadn't ridden north of Lake George since 1969, so the ride brought waves of nostalgia as I recalled the places my parents took me as we drove up to Canada every summer in the 1950s (don't get the idea that I was this "rich little kid" who was sent to camp every summer. On the contrary, my mom saw an ad in a local paper for a kiddie-land director in a camp in Canada, applied and got the job. I went for free).

    It seems that we'd just missed a torrential downpour after our quick stop in Lewis, New York, as the Northway was soaking wet. We became victims of the wet roadway and the spray off passing cars, which drenched us but only from the knees down. Thank G-D for the sun. You know, that lucky old sun, that ain't got nothin' to do but roll around in the sky all day? Well, it shone brightly on us and we soon dried off.

    We got to the border, were asked some fairly innocuous questions by the Canadian customs agent and rode off into Quebec. My heart was pounding as we rode over the Champlain Bridge into downtown Montreal. We rode around for about 15 minutes and pulled up to the door of the hotel. Sounds like the norm? Not in this case. It was the evening of Canada Day, and the week of the Montreal Jazz Festival. Hotel rooms were non-existent. My guardian angel intervened and we got lucky: a room for two nights in a wonderful hotel that even had an indoor garage.

The face on the doorman was priceless as we pulled up and unloaded the bike (he thought we'd stopped to ask directions). It's not that there aren't plenty of bikes there, there are. There just aren't many fat, old, colorful, noisy Harleys, ridden by an old hippie and his wife. What made this even funnier was that the front door of the hotel we pulled up to was that of The Ritz Carlton.

CHAPTER 11
In Montreal--Still 2001

It felt good to wash up, and lie down for a quickie (now, now, that's a nap), but after a very short power snooze I wanted to reconnect with old friends.
"Do you think any of your old buddies still live here, or are even alive," I thought as I thumbed through the phone book? I'd know soon enough.

Old camp songs flew through my mind as I opened the phone book. Silly songs, funny songs, old rock and roll (especially the slow songs that allowed you to walk over to a girl and ask her to dance–if you had the nerve), and songs in foreign languages; I'm smiling just sitting here thinking about it as I write.
My mind drifted to one of the great 'loves' of my life at camp –I not only remember her name (Doreen) but her face as well--I was 12 years old.
"As I lie awake, resting from the day, I can hear the clock passing time away. Oh, I couldn't sleep 'cause on my mind, was the image of the girl I had to find…"
I'm not even sure if the words are right but the song, Image of a Girl, was one of those slow ones. Ooooo eeeeeeeeee baby, my mind was racing.

With the phone book open on my bed, I started to search. The first name was Teddy Matthews.

Teddy's parents owned the camp and he was like my older brother (you know what I mean, he could kick the crap out of you but G-D forbid anybody else touch you...). He was home and couldn't believe his ears, nor me mine. We decided to get together the next afternoon for a quick drink--it'd been a long time and a drink might've been more than enough. Who knew!

I made four more calls and got responses that still bring a tear to my eye. Everybody wanted to get together (although time constraints didn't allow for it). It was intense, to say the least. I laugh now recalling the response once they knew it was me, "umm ... uh... uh... is... uh..." I would jump in and say: "She's gonna be 86 in two weeks, yes she's fine." Since they all knew my mother from working at Camp Bayview, and they thought she was old in the 50s, they were afraid to ask if my mother was still alive.

Bobby, I found out, no longer lived in Montreal; he lived in Toronto. Hell, we were heading there anyway, and I really wanted to see him again, so I called.
Bobby picked up the phone: "Hello?"
"Hey Bobby," I said, "it's been a long time."
"Yes it has," he answered. "Tell me, do you still say your prayers before you go to bed?"
I couldn't imagine how he knew who was on the other end of the phone, but his question was legitimate. I never went to sleep without saying my prayers. At home, my father would sit on the edge of the bed and we'd recite The Sh'ma: "Sh'ma Yisrael Adonai Eloheynu Adonai

From Cross To Cross

Echad." Hear O Israel The Lord is our G-D the Lord in One. It is the watchword of Judaism and the first acknowledgment of monotheism in organized religion. I recited the Sh'ma every night at camp as well.

What I didn't know then was that it is also the prayer you say, if you can, before death-- that along with a confessional. So, obviously, if you die in your sleep you've covered your bases, so to speak.

There is no question that was copied with: "now I lay me down to sleep, I pray the Lord my soul to keep. If I die before I wake, I pray the Lord my soul to take." Sounds pretty much like covering one's bases to me.

In any case it was going to be a few days before we got to Toronto and we were going to enjoy Montreal.

Montreal is a gorgeous city although my eyes might've been clouded by the waves of nostalgia that swept over me, and riding those streets, many of which brought us back to a different era, was joyous. I'm not just talking about my nostalgia; I'm talking about a city with grace and charm. A city that is as modern as it is quaint and charming, with beautiful old homes, many of them mansions, directly across the street from new high-rise apartment buildings. You can ride up Mount Royal from where you can see the city: Old Montreal, the port, the Olympic Stadium, St. Joseph's; I could go on and on.

Shelly and I rode all over the city on Sunday, this was, of course, after I went out that morning to get bagels. Don't laugh but every Sunday morning I go out and bring home bagels (okay, laugh). This Sunday, Sunday in Montreal, we were going to sit down to a nice, hot breakfast.

Piero, the concierge, seeing that we were from the New York City area, asked if we liked bagels and told us that the BEST bagels in the world were in Montreal.
"You never heard of St. Viateur bagels," he asked.
"Nope," I said.
After giving me a five-minute song and dance I had no choice, so the next morning I rode to St. Viateur and bought bagels (I bought some for him, too).
Riding down to St. Viateur brought me back to the shtetlach in Poland and the Ukraine in the mid to late 1930s.

Photographer Roman Vishniac in one of his photo books, A Vanished World, captures what is still the world here. Shops' signs were in Yiddish (and, of course, French), and the men dressed as their ancestors, no, as our ancestors, with long coats and round short brimmed hats. Even the young children coming from or going to cheder wore small versions of the same outfit. G-D, you look through this photo-essay and see it all over again, sixty five years later; fifty five years after the end of the war, the end of six million of our people and ask why! They are right; one picture is worth a thousand words.

Two young boys stared at me. I was stopped at a light, the throatiness of my engine breaking whatever silence there might have been. They couldn't take their eyes off of me. I turned, looked at them, and in the best Yiddish I knew said: "Vus kiktsuch?" (what are you looking at?) They had no idea what to make of me and just stood there, mouths agape, as the light turned green and I rode away.

From Cross To Cross

We rode through the city and hung out with a couple of R.C.M.P. for a bit--they wanted to talk--it's amazing how warm most people are with bikers. Of course, as they walked over to us I heard the lyrics "... it increases my paranoia, like looking in the mirror and seeing a police car...", but I was wrong. One didn't speak English very well but the four of us hung out talking about bikes; they both rode.

Did I mention a weird rattle coming from my engine? No? A rattle, from the engine of a Harley? "...hmmmmm why should today be any different..." I thought, recounting Tevye from Fiddler on the Roof. "A rattle from the engine of a Harley!! Sounds crazy, no? but in our little society of Harleyville, one might say that every one of our bikes has some rattle or another. You may ask why do you stay in Harleyville if there are so many rattles? We stay because Harleyville is our home..."

The rattle, as I examined the bike, was the bracket under the exhaust that, obviously, came loose during the trip up, and after searching for an open 'any-store' (remember it was Canada Day, not to mention Sunday-- can you find an open hardware store on July fourth in the USA?) we found a hardware store, thanks to the RCMP, bought nuts, bolts, and washers and made a quick repair.

The ride around Montreal was wonderful but it started to pour so we parked the bike, grabbed an umbrella from the front desk of our hotel and walked around downtown.

Oh, the bagels? They were okay! What do you expect from a kid who grew up eating bagels at the source, Brooklyn?

We walked around downtown Montreal in the rain, stopped at a coffee house and sat there for a while just to people watch: a great pastime no matter where you are.

The huge clock on the wall across the street jarred us back to reality. It was time to meet Teddy.

The section of Montreal where Teddy lives made it seem as if one were in the suburbs. No sooner did we turn off the main drag then there were no more stores, only homes, and unless you turned and looked behind, you'd have no idea that you were still in the middle of a major city.

We pulled into the driveway and Teddy, obviously hearing the bike, came out. Fifty eight, I'm talking about Teddy's age not mine, doesn't look like sixteen or seventeen, but his smile was infectious just the same, and after a huge bear hug, Shelly and I walked in.

It was supposed to be a couple of drinks, but Teddy's wife, Elaine, had all kinds of hors d'oeuvres ready and the girls drank wine while Teddy and I downed a couple of glasses of Scotch.

We talked about camp, about his parents' home on the lake, and we talked about the house in Montreal that he grew up in and the opulent way in which they lived. We laughed, we cried and we reminisced for hours. They threw a bunch of stuff on the grill, called for a delivery of pommes frittes (french fries) and we ate, and we ate... We didn't think we'd stay for dinner, remember what I said about a drink being more than enough, but obviously I couldn't have been more wrong. We went on and on and on--it was great.

From Cross To Cross

    Teddy and I lit up cigars out on the deck while the girls ducked inside; it was getting a bit chilly. Ted grabbed a phone asked me to dial my mom and then the two of them talked until they laughed and they cried; it was tremendous. We said our goodbyes with huge hugs and promises of keeping in touch. Shelly and I mounted up and headed back to the hotel; it was eleven thirty.

    The next morning we loaded up and headed the bike northwest towards the Laurentian Mountains.

CHAPTER 12
Still 2001--Going Back to Camp

It was a cold Canadian morning as we rode up toward camp by way of Ste. Agathe, and many of the towns we passed jogged my memory. Ste. Agathe was where one of our rival camps was located and we spent plenty of time there playing inter-camp games. It was also the only big town on the way to Camp Bayview. We ate breakfast there, and headed down the back roads (there's nothing else) heading for St. Donat.

This area is breathtaking. The lakes are crystal clear and bluer than blue, and the Laurentian Mountains are one of the oldest mountain ranges in North America; from what I understand, the rounder the peaks the older the range.

St. Donat was a one block town (ok, so maybe it was two blocks) and we'd go into town occasionally for pommes frittes at a little restaurant called Charbonneau's. Well, we rode into St. Donat and it is no longer a one block town, au contraire, it is very built up with tons of stores and coffee shops, restaurants and more tourists than I remember seeing all eleven years that I was there combined. The whole area had changed. Part of that is the result of the passing of forty years and the other the massive construction in the Mont Tremblant region spilling out and affecting towns for miles.

St. Donat's new size didn't allow for any reminiscing and I had no desire to stop anyway, so we rode through and out of town. I wasn't sure if I'd know where to turn off for the camp; boy was I wrong. There it was, a dirt road then and a dirt road still--it called to me and I turned onto it.

I could see Lac Archambault through the trees, my eyes started to fill with tears and I could hardly catch my breath. We passed lots of homes, all were on the lake, and I remembered Teddy's folk's house. How could I forget it, it was my second home, 'my' summerhouse albeit for a couple of weeks before camp started and after camp was over. More so, back then it was the only house there and now it isn't there anymore. I can still see every inch of it, at least in my mind's eye.

I see the Pine trees that lined the road and the entrance to the house. I remember the size of the property and I can see how far it spread all along the lake. I see the boat house which housed an elegant Chris Craft, all mahogany and brass, and teddy's parents always in white: commodore caps, shirts, slacks, socks and white bucks.

I see the house itself with the moose heads and elk heads adorning the walls. There were gun racks, bearskin rugs, and a wooden propeller, oh my, the memories were flooding my brain and I had to stop. As I write this my eyes fill up all over again and I have to stop as well.

You have to understand that this was my childhood, a place that I looked forward to all year--NO, that doesn't express it. I lived the entire year dreaming about being up in the Laurentians, on Lac Archambault, at Camp Bayview.

The horses we rode; Blackie, Queenie, and King and others leased for the camp season, and I remember Prince, the huge draft horse pulling a wagon all around the camp. They used the wagon for picking up garbage and moving things from place to place. I can still hear Old monsieur Richer, with his leather face and infectious smile who drove the wagon–"whoa Prince," he would say (with his accent, prince sounds like prance); oh yes, I still hear it.

The sides of the road to camp were still dotted with blueberry bushes and I remembered the many times our bunk would walk down the road picking them and then bringing them back to Mary, the baker. I can still smell the fresh, hot, blueberry pie we'd fill up on at night. I turned right onto a smaller dirt road and saw the bunks through the trees in the distance. The cabins were still red and white just as they'd been forty one years earlier.

The first building was administration and after taking a couple of minutes to compose myself, I walked in.

It's kind of hard to sneak up on someone when your Thunderheaders let people know you're coming a half mile before you get there, so waiting outside the administration building wouldn't have made a lot of sense.

The director understood that I'd been a camper there many years ago and he had no problem if Shelly and I walked around.

There were some changes, DUH, but the laughter of kids playing transcends everything. The bunks were the same, the boulders that we slid down hadn't gotten any smaller and these kids were sliding down them as well. The saying "When I was small and Christmas trees were tall…now I am tall and Christmas trees are small…" didn't work here. I was small and tall that very instant.

The language had changed. When I went the camp was all Anglo and now it was all French.

We walked down to the lake, and here was the biggest change. Archambault is a huge lake, the camp is on one of the bays, and this bay is about a mile and a half across.

I was an excellent swimmer throughout my childhood and from the time I was seven years old, I would swim that lake. When I was nine I decided to swim across the lake and back. Bobby was going to swim across with me, get in the boat for the trip back and I'd swim the second half alone. He changed his mind, and decided he'd attempt the swim back. I dragged him the last one hundred yards or so.

When I was at Bayview there was nothing on the entire bay but the camp. We'd walk through the woods around the lake, make camp, pitch tents, dig a fire pit, a latrine and marvel at all that G-D had given us.

Sometimes we'd take rowboats or canoes to various parts of the lake (or surrounding lakes) and do the same. The other side of the lake had ice caves and we'd row across and climb the mountain to look in. It would be the middle of the summer and these caves were solid ice.

So there we stood, Shelly and I, looking out across the bay, the then pristine forest, now dotted with homes.

From Cross To Cross

We took a bunch of pictures and we walked back up the hill from the lake and peered into the buildings of Bayview. This was my summer life. It's where I used to play, dance, sing, fall in love, get my heart crushed—I'm sitting here chuckling as I remember and write--watching the faces of these kids doing the same while, in my head, playing back our time there. In the movie Camelot King Arthur says that "...the only true vacations are in the past..." I think he's right.
    The only difference is that I am still a kid--in my heart, head and soul if nowhere else.

    I wear a t-shirt on which is written: "I may grow older but I'll never grow up," and another that says, "I should be all grown up by now, I wonder what went wrong." My mom hates both of them.

    Shelly and I walked through the camp and headed back to the bike, reliving our individual camp experiences, each in his own thoughts. You see, we met at a camp in 1971 and people who've been to sleep-away camps share a certain bond and relive similar experiences even if their camps were on other sides of the world.
    The echoes of our laughter from forty years ago melded with that of these kids at play today and I felt a warm glow come over me. It was wonderful, it said it all, and I looked up and said thanks. It was a gift to have been able to have been there then, and another gift to be able to return now. Bayview shaped my life in many ways and left me with so many memories, not all wonderful, but all a part of my life, all pieces of my puzzle.

I sit here now with the words of one of my favorite songs, *In My Life*, by Lennon and McCartney, echoing in my head:

> There are places I'll remember
> all my life though some have changed.
> Some forever, not for better,
> some have gone and some remain.
>
> All these places had their moments
> with lovers and friends I still can recall.
> Some are dead and some are living.
> In my life I loved them all.

'NUFF SAID.

We got back on the bike and sat, for a moment more than necessary, allowing the throaty growl of the Thunderheaders to fill the air around Camp Bayview (now Camp St. Donat). I wanted to scream, for what would more than likely be my last time on that property: "Hey, I'm back, remember me? I missed you, thanks for everything, and good bye."

Shelly had her hands on my shoulders as we rode the old dirt road out of camp, I was glad we were there but it was time to move on. We headed back through St. Donat to Ste. Agathe, north to St. Jovite, took a turn off the highway and started a back roads ride through Southwestern Quebec.

CHAPTER 13
Headin' for Ontario–Still 2001

Route 323 in southwestern Quebec, is a two lane-- one in each direction--road, twists and turns as it winds its way Southwest. Charming villages, sparkling blue lakes and small mountains adorn this necklace-like road.

As we rode I spotted a motorcycle stopped, and I pulled over. "Are you OK?" I asked.

He motioned to me in a way that made me think he couldn't hear me. I repeated my query, this time many decibels higher. His response was the same. I shut the engine finally understanding that he couldn't hear me because of the pipes. When I asked for the third time he answered me in French; he didn't understand English. We all laughed as I made the OK sign with my thumb and forefinger and we rode off.

The further away one gets from the major cities the less English is spoken. Thank goodness that my French started coming back to me so that I could converse at, if nothing else, a base level. After a stop for gas and some thirst quenching liquids we headed for route 315, again two lanes one in each direction, continuing our ride towards Ottawa, the capital of the Province of Ontario.

Lenny Mandel

Shelly saw a road sign and tapped my shoulder to let me know that we'd missed the turn off. Of course I told her she was wrong, thought for a moment, decided that I didn't want to end up heading back towards Montreal, and stopped.

An elderly gentleman was sweeping out a garage and I asked about the route I was taking. He rattled off an answer, raised his arm as if to say bon voyage (good trip), and continued to sweep. Another major problem with the language is that in exurbia the patois is, sort of, squashed so that even French Canadians from other parts of the province may have a hard time understanding.

I guess he figured out that I didn't understand him: probably because I stood there grinning like an idiot. He was right. After a couple of minutes he explained to me that the road I wanted to take was all gravel. He used the word four or five times in the same sentence, and although the word is the same in both languages--a fact that I didn't know--I had no idea what he meant.

I began repeating; gravel, gravel? at which point he walked over to the side of the road, picked up a handful of gravel and said: "oui, gravel!" If you don't think that it's funny try saying the word with a heavy French accent three or four times quickly and see if you understand yourself (FYI the accent is on the vel. gra-VEL).

So we switched to 317, got onto 148 and rode over the Ottawa River Bridge into the capital city of Ottawa. We decided to turn off at the first possible exit and look for a place to eat, and as luck would have it, ended up in the center of the market area. There were hundreds of people and plenty of restaurants. We parked in front of one, sat on the porch overlooking the bike and ate.

The bike attracts quite a bit of attention, even standing still, and a bunch of people took pictures of it, asking permission to stand near it. My answer is always the same; "take the picture with her sitting on it, just be careful 'cause the pipes may be hot."
We ate a wonderful lunch and although we'd originally planned to spend a day or two in Ottawa, I was itching to get to Toronto and reunite with Bobby--need I say more.

Shelly and I decided to forego route 7 and make time getting to Toronto. We knew that even though 7 is a wonderful route it takes a long time if it's busy. So it was going to be the 416 to the 401 all the way through (In Ontario the roads are prefaced with the word-the. It seems to give the road character--I found out later that it's that way in California as well).
We were getting tired so we decided to spend the night in Kingston, get up early, and do the two hundred forty kilometers (about one hundred fifty miles) in two and one half hours, getting there before noon. It was the perfect plan. We'd check into the hotel, walk around Toronto for a few hours (including the Hockey Hall of Fame), relax for a bit and meet Bobby and his wife Nedda for dinner. You are familiar with the adage, "…the best laid plans…" right?
Well, we woke up in the morning, looked up at an overcast sky and as I unlocked the bike I ran my hand over the rear tire; it was bald. I was pretty sure I'd checked it before we left (DUH), oh, well. Luckily there

was a Harley dealer in Kingston and, amazingly, he was a mile from the motel. I rode over to the shop and Dale, the service manager, assured me he'd have me out of there in less than an hour. Great, we'd grab a quick breakfast at the motel, go back to the dealership, pack up the bike and go. It was all going to work out despite needing a new tire.

After breakfast we called Dale; "Oh, Lenny, I've been trying to reach you," he said. "It seems that when we took off the tire the sprocket fell off and we don't have one here to replace it."

I've been around Harleys for a long time and I've never heard of a sprocket falling off before but... "...a sprocket falling off of a Harley? Sounds crazy no? But in our little community of Harleyville..." There was Tevye from Fiddler on the Roof again.

We got to the dealership and Dale was calling around in search of a sprocket for my 1989 FLHS. In the meantime the mechanic was peening the sprocket back on to the wheel. Lady Luck smiled upon us; Davies Harley Davidson in Toronto had it and they were going to put it aside for me--oh joy, oh rapture.

All the while I was on the phone with Scott Covert, the lead tech at Liberty, Harley Davidson in Rahway, N.J. who was also a bit shocked at the sprocket story; he'd only seen it happen once before and he'd been an H-D mechanic for 15 years.

"Limp it in to Toronto," he said. "No whooping on the throttle, limp it in!"

It was 11 o'clock in the morning and I was not looking forward to a four hour drive down the 401 into Toronto, but the only other choice was to spend another night in Kingston. I could hear The Band echoing in my head, "...Oh Lord, I'm stuck out in Kingston again" (ok so they were stuck in Lodi). Limp we must, limp we did.

My idea of limping ended up being a fifty or sixty mph ride in the right lane of the 401, watching the signs of towns that we were passing, each bringing us closer and closer to our new sprocket in Toronto. We got there in about three hours and, of course, the dealership was many miles North of where we came in. It was the longest street in North America, a street with a traffic light on just about every corner and traffic to beat the band.

Bob Davies Harley Davidson in Richmond Hill, Ontario is a beautiful place. It wasn't exactly on the list of 'things you must see while in Toronto,' but I was overjoyed that we'd made it. The people there were great. They had the sprocket waiting for us. They went over the entire bike, fixed some problems--or possible future problems, sent us across the street for lunch (a late lunch but lunch nonetheless) and greeted us with wonderful smiles and warmth.

Chris, the young tech who worked on the bike showed me a couple of the things he'd taken care of, took the bike for a test ride and asked if it was for sale. It made me smile. My FL, which looks like an old, calm, ride has a one hundred four cubic inch motor, carburetor and head work by Jimmy Simpson, puts out over ninety Horsepower and over one hundred ft lbs of torque to the rear wheel. Stock it ain't!

It was past four o'clock, we still had to get to our hotel, which was in downtown Toronto, and guess what? It was rush hour. What a day. What the hell, we made it, we were safe, the bike was great and we had days more to ride.

At the hotel, I grabbed a quick shower and Shelly hung out in the bathtub for about an hour.

Eric Saibil, the older brother of the crush of my youth, also lives in Toronto and when he found out that we were going to be there wanted to meet as well. There are so many kids (well, ex-kids) and counselors all over Canada, and the USA as well, that maybe it would be better to have a reunion; see how many 'Bayviewers' there are, try to round them up and have one huge party.

If you thought that I was excited about meeting Teddy I was that and more to see Bobby Lash. He'd kept in contact with us the entire ride from Montreal and his sense of humor hadn't changed. He still had this very dry, sarcastic and clever way about him that always made me laugh, and I'd been smiling thinking of what he'd be like after all these years. I didn't have very long to wait.

CHAPTER 14
Bobby and Nedda

Bobby and Nedda pulled up to our hotel in a big silver Cadillac, which makes perfect sense--he also rides a Gold Wing (I was making fun of it then, but I ride one now). We were waiting for them at the entrance and it was quite a scene. He jumped out, and uncharacteristically, as I found out later, gave me this great big bear hug. Understand that both Bob and I are pretty big bears anyway. We were all smiles and it felt as if we'd never been apart.

The four of us supped in a wonderful little bistro in downtown Toronto. We ate way too much, we drank too much (the girls didn't so we didn't worry about designated drivers), and once again filled the air with raucous laughter and, of course, a smattering of tears.

Life, as fragile as it is--and isn't it though--is to be lived. Not just to take a sip from the cup, on the contrary, to drink deeply and fully for as long as you can.

We drove around Toronto that night, stopped for coffee and made plans to meet for breakfast. Bob figured that after breakfast we'd hop on the bikes and we'd do some exploring around the outskirts of Toronto. That was fine by me.

The day broke overcast with a chance of showers (I thought that most prognosticators tell you that it would be dark followed by light—sorry, once again I couldn't resist). Bob and Nedda rode up on their wing, which is turquoise with a windshield the size of Kansas. Moreover, Bobby installed an oversized windshield wiper (electric, of course) as well, and whenever we stopped it was the topic of conversation with every biker we encountered. There are no windshield wipers on motorcycles! Not only that but he had lights installed on his wing that made it look like a Wurlitzer juke box when lit up at night. Off we rode.

I won't go into the ride in depth, but we stopped for a soda and rode some glorious back roads while watching three funnel clouds, not so far in the distance.

Seeing a tornado on television is one thing, but watching one creeping in your direction is a completely different experience; like get me outta here! Later we found out that the tornado touched down at the spot where we'd just stopped for sodas.

I can't even tell you what it felt like seeing Bobby after all those years. The exact same grin plastered across his face, the exact same face, albeit an older version.

It was wonderful, and that's how, after so many years, I finally hooked up with Bobby again.

Back to 2003, the rain finally started letting up as we continued riding southbound on route 221. Still in North Carolina, we were heading for Tennessee, but not before we rode up the mountain into Blowing Rock.

CHAPTER 15
Blowing Rock, N.C.

Blowing Rock is an artsy community, nestled high in the mountains of North Carolina, and I'm told, by my friend Sandy Newman (he refers to himself as 'white shoes Newman' because he lives in Miami) that it's a summer retreat for Miami 'Yiddlach' who want to escape the heat. That's probably why many of the license plates that we saw there were from Florida.

You ride in and out of the town itself rather quickly, and when you leave town you are riding through gorgeous forests along the top of the mountain: no Churches and no Crosses up here. Bob and Nedda took their time but Shelly and I picked up speed riding the curves through the forest.

The smell of pine, and the new grass, intensified by the recent rain, made me feel heady. It was incredible. It was exactly what I wanted to be doing and I felt a bit sad when we started descending, knowing we were heading for civilization--well, civilization for down there.

Halfway down the mountain, the road plateau'd and we waited for Bob to catch up. I had to pee so badly my eyeballs were floating (remember the all liquid diet with as much fluids as you can drink?) but the right side of the road was cliff. Bob and Nedda pulled up just as I was jumping through the high grass on the up-side of the road.

They smiled knowingly and off we rode again down the hill stopping at the gas station at the park's end.

We take lots of breaks, probably every seventy five minutes or so by the afternoon, just to kick out our cramping old legs and move our creaking bones. The rain had subsided to less than a drizzle but after this rest we were going to attempt Asheville with no more stops.

Bob had one proviso for picking places to stay: a swimming pool, and each one, so far, had one. If the days were warm, sunny and beautiful, we'd have no problem stopping at a river, lake or stream, throwing on swimsuits (or not) and hanging out in the water, but not on this trip. So after a day's ride Bob and I would hit the pool for thirty to forty five minutes. Water- I've felt comfortable in and around water my whole life. It is a soothing, relaxing world that brings you back to the most peaceful time: the womb. I don't remember the womb but I hear that it's a terrific place.

We were lifeguards when the girls wanted to know who the lifeguards were and we always let them climb up on the lifeguard chair to sit with us.

> *A grandmother and her grandson were playing at the water's edge at Brighton Beach when a wave came and took the grandson out to sea.*
> *She was screaming for help at the top of her lungs and, the lifeguard seeing this, jumped off the*

tower, ran through the sand, dove into the surf and swam at break-neck speed toward the little boy. He got him just as the boy was going under and carried him safely to shore.
Grandma was in tears: "Thank you, oh thank you, I will never be able to repay you for this, never. Please if there's anything that you ever need it's yours."
Holding her grandson in her arms, she looked up at the lifeguard and said: "Excuse me, he had a hat."

Route 221 continued its curvy ways, and its multitude of Churches out of North Carolina, into Tennessee and we left 221 to hop on route 40, the Interstate.

After the day of riding back roads, seventy miles an hour (actually eighty) on a super-highway was a treat. The fact that it stopped raining as well didn't hurt. We were in our glory.

Nine years had gone by since my first trip to Asheville for The National H.O.G. rally in 1994, and now I was back: this time with Shelly, Bob and Nedda. We parked the bikes, checked into our motel, Bob and I grabbed bathing suits and headed for the pool.

Chapter 16
Asheville, North Carolina
Days Three and Four

Later that evening we were directed to The Boat House, a nice restaurant on the edge of a lake about a mile from our motel, to have dinner. We got dressed and rode over.

It was exciting for a couple of reasons: it was an upscale restaurant, and we were going to eat outside, overlooking the lake; we love dining al-fresco. No such luck. The outdoor section was full and, much to Shelly's chagrin, we were forced to sit inside. As luck would have it----or is everything really bashert---the sky opened up and all the patrons sitting outside 'un-al-frescoed' it very quickly.

Dinner was great but it started raining again, so we waited, hoping the rain would stop before we rode back to the motel. The sky was dark with no sign of stars or moon; tropical storm Bill, or as women gleefully refer to it--'the himicane'--was heading our way.

When the sky is bright and the night filled with stars we ride with alacrity. No such luck on this trip.

The weather kept us glued to the Weather

Channel, and we knew that it'd be getting mighty wet the next couple of days as 'Bill' was about to engulf Eastern Tennessee and Western North Carolina. Bob and I checked the weather, knew the storm was about to beat the crap out of us, looked at each other and jumped into action. We cancelled our room reservations for the next two nights, made a reservation to stay where we were one extra night, and rented a car.

We figured that while in Asheville we'd visit Biltmore, the Vanderbilt estate, and check out the local hangouts. It's a hip town, reminiscent of Greenwich Village in the 60's, with cafes that have poetry readings and folk singers: very cool stuff.
On the way to the estate I told Bob that the Vanderbilts were actually Jews who fled the pogroms of Eastern Europe in the 1800s, came to America via Holland, assimilated into the culture, and amassed a fortune. It was meant as a joke until the first part of our guided tour through the house. Actually the Vanderbilt family name was Bilt (Van-from, der-the, bilt-build or builders—I translated it into—from the Bilt family) . I almost fell on the floor when I heard it.
Bilt was the maiden name of my paternal grandmother and her parents were wealthy landowners and dairy farmers in Poland. Their land was confiscated and they were all killed in the Holocaust, but they were the Bilts. I started to believe the line I handed Bobby and wondered how I could claim my share of this estate. No, just kidding. I think.

Although very informative, after a while the tour became tedious. I could've walked the estate in half the time and there was plenty that I would've liked to have seen and heard about that was never mentioned.

On the first floor there was a sitting room with three huge tapestries on the wall. They are Flemish, date back to the sixteenth century, and are all that remain of the seven original pieces called The Triumph of the Seven Virtues. The middle tapestry of the three had me mesmerized. It was filled with characters from the Bible.

The left side of the piece depicted biblical characters from the Old Testament, while the right side depicted characters from the New Testament. Atop the pillar on the right side was a woman, cross held high, benevolence and mercy shining around her. Atop the pillar on the left side of the tapestry was Moses (or Aaron) holding the Ten Commandments upside down in his right hand and the staff that he held was broken just below the banner. It depicted the defeat of the old and the joy of the new. It was blatantly anti-Semitic and I couldn't take my eyes off of it.

> *Henry Ford, a well known Anti-Semite, was approached by three Jews, Cohen, Schwartz and Goldstein who told him they had an invention that would make him a fortune. They called it air-conditioning and told him that it would allow people drive all through the summer in comfort.*
> *After being shown its virtues Ford agreed to buy their invention, but there was a proviso.*
> *"Every air conditioner that goes into your*
> *cars has to have our names on it," they said.*
> *Ford replied: "are you nuts, Cohen, Schwartz and Goldstein on my cars? No way."*

"No problem," they replied, "we'll go to General Motors."
Ford would never allow that so he made the deal. It was millions of dollars and the names of those three Jews are on every air conditioner made. That's right: Hi, Max and Norm.

I know what you're thinking and the answer is NO! I do not see anti-Semites hiding behind every bush. I am very conscious of who I am and where I come from and I am a constant reminder to myself that no Holocaust, no matter where, no matter against whom, should ever happen again.

Why does it piss Christians off that Jews don't have a problem being Jewish? Leave us alone and let us pray in our own way. No, that's not what it's all about. How much Christianity was brought on the people by force? Think about it. The Crusades: look at the root of the word crus=cross--the mission to make people worship the cross. The Inquisition; need I go further?

How many people have been killed in the name of G-D? How many were killed for not converting? How many have been killed by Jews for not wanting to be Jewish, any? Both questions are rhetorical--history is the witness.

When Mel Brooks' and Carl Reiner's 2000 year old man was asked if he ever manufactured anything he said that he used to manufacture the Magen David: the six pointed star. He employed six men, each with a point. They'd run at each other and when they came together they made the star.

From Cross To Cross

He was asked if he ever thought of manufacturing anything else and he said that once a man named Paul came to him. Paul said that he had a winner. It was going to be a big seller. It was called a cross. The 2000 year old man realized that he would only need two people and bang, you've got a cross.

"I looked at it, I turned it over and said it's simple, too simple," he said. "I didn't know then that it was eloquent."

In Ron Elisha's play "Two," which takes place in post-war Germany, Rabbi Chaim Levi, in speaking to Anna, a gentile woman who has come to him explains:

"...You know what the Star of David is in Hebrew? 'Magen David'-'Shield of David.' For him it was an emblem, a coat of arms emblazoned on his shield, and with it he raged into battle and was victorious. (While he points to the yellow star armband, he continues) Now see what has become of it.

Therein lies the success of the Christian peoples. We, we Jews, we took a shield, a symbol of strength and of pride and of security and turned into the cross of our suffering, the symbol of our abject humiliation, the face of death itself. Whereas you, you Christians, you took the cross, an implement of torture and of suffering and of death, and turned into a symbol of salvation."

I thought about the Jews, centuries and centuries of Jews who faced death, were maimed, tortured and killed but wouldn't succumb; wouldn't bow down and worship idols or false G-Ds. I thought of the Marranos in fifteenth century Spain who practiced Christianity above ground and Judaism in their basements so that they wouldn't be burned at the stake. How many of them fled to Italy, Portugal and Holland, and how many of their progeny, all these centuries later, are now devout Catholics?

    I thought of Rabbi Akiva who lived around the time of Christ. The Romans forbade the teaching of Torah but Akiva chose to continue despite the severest of penalties if he were caught. He was led to his death and as they scraped off his skin with iron combs he recited Sh'ma Yisrael Adonai Eloheynu Adonai Echad, the watchword of monotheism.
    His disciples queried why he was reciting it then and he replied; "All my life I have been troubled by the verse 'Love the Lord your G-D with all your heart and with all your soul' which means if He were to take your life. I often wondered if I'd ever be able to fulfill that obligation and now I can." He passed from this world saying, "The Lord is One."

    The early Christians were Romans at heart and followed the ways of their Roman upbringing. It was much easier to force someone to do as you say with the threat of death than with reason. My blood boiled standing at that tapestry looking at the denigration, once again, of the basis of their own beliefs. It must be so easy!

    I finished the tour and was happy to be outside. I envied these Christians, the ease with which they followed the path of 'truth.' Why is it that theirs is the only truth? It's not a very 'Christian' ideal, putting to death all of those who disagree or don't want to follow the path. What happened to benevolence? What happened to love thy neighbor as thyself?

Chapter 17
Day four mid-day

We lunched at The Bistro, a lovely little restaurant at the Biltmore Winery, and I decided to stray from the diet and eat; the vodka martini I had to start the meal was the topper.

I needed a change, I needed to 'make a l'chayim'--a toast. Tevye drinks with his, almost, future son-in-law Lazar Wolf, the butcher. Not only do they 'make a l'chayim,' they sing l'chayim. It was an intense morning. My thoughts were all over the place and I needed to take the edge off.

When you haven't really eaten solid foods (salads notwithstanding) for a week or eight days, a glass of vodka hits you much more quickly than usual; it felt great. Lunch was scrumptious. After we ate, we took a quick tour of the winery--and what tour would be complete without a wine tasting, we left.

The eight thousand acre estate, originally 100,000 acres, is beautiful--hey, the house alone is four acres--and we drove around and through until we reached the exit.

Two of my father's favorite expressions were: "rich or poor, it's good to have money," and, "it's better to be rich and healthy than poor and sick." I smiled thinking that all through the trip. My dad also used to say that if everybody sat around a huge table and everybody put all of their 'problems' on that table, each and every one would take his own back.

It comes back to him telling me not to put too much emphasis on money.

"Money," he would say, "is round, and as quickly as it rolls to you it can roll away from you."

I remember being told that Sugar Ray Robinson once said: "I really don't care about money, but it sure quietens my nerves." I said it before, we never had much money, sometimes none, but growing up in my home, the money was love.

It was Passover, either 1955 or 1956 and I was eight or nine, the first time I had an inkling of how bad things were for us financially.

Passover in our home was tons of work, but it was amazing. We cleaned the apartment; it seemed like it took forever. We removed all the Passover dishes, utensils and cookware from the tops of myriad closets and washed everything; the dishes, utensils and cookware we used the rest of the year were packed away (remember we had two sets of everything, dairy and meat).

> G-D said to Moses: "Thou shalt not cook a kid in its mother's milk."
> Moses thought for a while and said; "Oh, Oh, I get it. You want us to eat meat and dairy separately."

> G-D said to Moses: "Listen, Moses all I'm saying is thou shalt not cook a kid in its mother's milk."
> Moses thought for a long while and said; "Oh, Oh, I get it. I really get it. You want us to have separate plates, knives, forks, spoons, dishes and cookware for dairy meals and for meat meals."
> G-D said: "Moses, Moses just listen to what I'm saying. Thou shalt not cook a kid in its mother's milk."
> Moses, despondent, sat in thought for a long while and finally, as if a light clicked on, he jumped up and said; "Oh, Oh, I get it, no, no, I get it, I really, really get it. You want us to wait six hours after eating meat to eat dairy."
> G-D looked down and said: "Moses, do whatever you want."

My mother sent me down to the avenue to pick up a few items that we needed for the first two days of the holiday. So I ran down to Waldbaum's and, while walking in the Kosher for Passover food aisle, saw this really cute Passover box. I don't remember what was in it but I thought that it would be a cute addition to our Seder table. The Seder is the festive meal where we recall the exodus from Egypt; Jesus' last supper was a Seder. The word Seder means order, and everything is done in a specific order.

I got home, put the grocery bags on the floor and gave my mother the change. I was so excited and couldn't wait to see the look on her face when she saw my surprise. She looked at the money and asked me where the rest was. I'd never been asked that question before:

so much for the surprise. I reached into the bag, pulled out the box and my mother began screaming. I don't remember it being more than a couple of dollars but the tears running down her cheek and the pain in her voice stopped me cold.

She had completely budgeted for the Holiday and I screwed it up by spending money that we didn't have. Crying hysterically I told her I'd go back to the avenue and return it, I was sorry and didn't know that things were so bad. At that moment the fact that I knew there was a problem, made my mother more upset than the problem itself. The thing I bought? We kept it.

Passover was really a joy in our home and my parents made sure that all our friends and relatives that didn't make a Seder would be at ours. I can't remember a Seder in our apartment with less than twenty or thirty guests; a four-and-one-half room apartment (I never figured out which the half room was, but that's what the apartment was called) with all those people, and we had a Seder each night for two nights.

Michael and Jimmy, my cousins who lived outside of Boston, spent their Passover/Easter and Christmas vacations with us (in my house they were called spring and mid-winter vacations). They were my brothers three times a year and being at my house was lots of fun; it also gave their mother a break.

We all slept in my room. It was crowded but great, and Michael would tell scary stories. Michael loved to scare me.

It was the night before the first Seder and Michael was telling us the story of the man who walked the streets at night preying on young boys and girls. He would break into their apartments, wait for them in the dark and then chop them into little pieces. By the time the cops got to the scene there was blood everywhere and finger tips, knuckles, toes, a severed head and on and on and on. They called him the butcher. I lay my head down on my pillow and there was a knock on the front door. I heard my mom ask who was there and I heard a voice on the other side of the door: "it's the butcher." I hid under the covers while Michael roared with laughter.

It wasn't a set-up; the butcher was delivering my mother's meat order for the holiday.

The first night of Passover came and people began arriving. No food was allowed in our house that we didn't buy ourselves so people brought flowers, a gift, or they brought nothing. All the furniture in the living room was either pushed to the side or moved into my parents' bedroom and we lined tables up end to end all the way into the den. Each table was not only a different shape and size they were all different heights. The trick was not to put a place setting near the abutting tables: the wine glasses were even trickier.

The Seders were wonderful and they got better every year. My dad sat at the head of this long string of tables and we read the Haggadah from cover to cover, going around the table with every person participating. If you couldn't read Hebrew, you read in English, and there were exceptions that broke the order of going around the table where my dad did specific parts, and the kids did specific parts. We had plenty of non-Jews at our Seders over the years and they participated as well. There were no exceptions to the participation rule.

To this day I can smell the apartment: the soup, the roast and all. I see the candles burning bright and I can hear the laughter and singing that continued way into the night as well.

There's a point in the Seder where we open the door to let the prophet Elijah in the house, and there's a cup of wine set aside specifically for him. My mom went to the door, opened it and the mops and brooms that we propped up against it fell with a crash. Mom jumped and we cracked up.

When I was very young my father would gently nudge the table so that the wine in Elijah's cup would shake.

"You see," he'd say, "Elijah's drinking." I didn't understand how he wasn't blasted silly after a dozen homes; forget about one hundred thousand.

Passover is very different for us now as we no longer make the Seder in our home; we go away. There came a time when it became a chore for my folks to schlep the dishes and clean the house. We decided that it would be more fun to have someone else do the work, after all this is the holiday that celebrates freedom, going from slavery to freedom; slaving in the kitchen doesn't exactly fit the spirit of the holiday. Here's the way I expressed my feelings about what celebrating Pesach is all about, when asked by a member of my congregation:

"Well, it's almost Pesach," I said. I look forward to spending these eight days, as I'm sure you all do, with my family and extended family. This year we will be reveling

From Cross To Cross

on the white sand beaches of Tahiti, swimming in the azure waters of the Pacific along with the dolphins.

Picture it: a Seder under the palm trees reading the Haggadah by the light of flaming torches, the dark night sparkling with the lights of its jewels--the stars and the moon. The natives stand staring at us with awe, and wonder at the strange language we are speaking and the even stranger rituals we follow. We need salt water so that we can dip the potatoes, and a bare-footed server runs to the ocean's edge scooping salt water from the sea with a Conch shell, pure white.

At our Seder we, the youngest from each family unit, stand and recite the four questions. It's an interesting sight. My mom is the youngest of five children, and at 86 she stands, as do I, my son Wayne, his friend Jeff (who is six feet five inches tall) and so on until we get to the youngest at our Seder table who is now about seventeen. We are about thirty one people singing together and reciting different parts of the Haggadah as we go around the table. We've made changes to our Seder, adding stories and songs making the experience more than just tradition.

The natives standing around, smiling as we sing: Take Me Out To The Seder (to the tune of Take Me Out To The Ball Game) and There's No Seder Like Our Seder (to the tune of There's No Business Like Show Business). Our sons and daughters, mostly grown, some already married or engaged, one with four children of her own, and all beautiful inside and out, create their own wonderful spirituality with the boisterous singing and laughter.

When we drink each glass of wine, and we drink four (at least) full cups, one of the boys will start by saying: "all right, everybody leeeeeeean to the left." It is joyous and we notice that more natives than are supposed to be there have come onto the beach to watch these rituals.

Dressed to the nines, we are. Suits, white shirts and ties, beautiful dresses, shined shoes, each man wearing a kipah, some sitting on pillows, all of this in diametric opposition to the bare-chested, bare-foot natives that are now surrounding our table.

"Kol dichphin yetay v'yechol. Kol ditzrich yetay v'yiphsach." All who are hungry come and eat. All who are needy come and celebrate the Pesach. Hmmm, do we invite the natives to our feast, to partake in our Seder?

Now there are canoes; beautifully painted outriggers paddled by a dozen men that pull up and onto the beach. The man who comes up to me is obviously the chief. Tattoos adorn his body and, although without bright colors, they speak volumes.

We invite him to join us and we explain the symbols and the rituals that we are enjoying. We talk about slavery, the Exodus from Egypt, the bitter herbs, the charoset, shank bone and egg, and he nods as if he understands.

We eat gefilte fish, and I explain about this, the craftiest, most cunning and hardest fish to catch—the Gefilte—and why it is such a delicacy. The kids have all heard this story before (every time any one comes up and asks me about gefilte fish) and do their best to keep straight faces. I explain that the Gefilte is easily spooked when nervous and if it sees a glimmer of metal under the water it turns inside itself, coming out on its own other side (the head now emerging from where there was a tail) and swims away.

The natives begin to dance, a chorus of men around this huge fire, and we join them creating circles into circles into circles, the sand as soft as talcum powder under our, now, bare feet.
We go back to the table, say Birkat Hamazon and move steadily towards Chad Gadya, the last song in the Haggadah. The fire on the beach has diminished to glowing embers as we sing. It is getting very late, and most of the natives have already left.
We look out over the still and silent Pacific still glowing with the lights of the heavenly bodies above, and we know that in the morning, after Shul, we'll be frolicking in that beautiful blue sea, eating fresh coconuts, and enjoying each other. We sit there and recount stories of Pesachs past, and talk about those of us who are no longer with us to enjoy and be enjoyed. They're there just the same.

It's the sharing. It's being part of a joyous, joyful time. It's families that have grown together after spending eighteen years together each Pesach. It's watching our kids grow and have kids of their own. It's the singing and the laughter and the tears. We are families from New York, New Jersey, Detroit, St. Louis, Memphis and Chicago. We are one fabulous family although only units are related by blood.
All the feelings and emotions, the rituals and songs I speak about are all true. Tahiti? Tahiti is a figment of my

Pesach imagination (James Taylor was going to Carolina—in his mind) but then where you are when you celebrate this glorious time, is only a state of mind: the one you put yourself in when you create the mood and surround yourself with those you truly love.
Now that's what celebrating joyous occasions should be all about."

The way our families met and became involved is a pretty cool story as well.
Our Pesach trips were just us, our immediate family: my parents, Shelly, Wayne, and me. Occasionally other cousins would join us on our trips, and various in-laws showed up a couple of years; these trips weren't mundane. We went to different sections of Puerto Rico, Nassau, The Bahamas, Paradise Island, The Dominican Republic, up and down both coasts of Florida, Israel and now you can have a Pesach vacation (and I mean a kosher trip) almost anywhere in the world.

Our 'immediate family only' trips came to a halt in 1984, while celebrating Pesach in Aruba along with a bunch of other small groups of family units. Seated on the other side of the room from us was a family from St. Louis, and in one corner another family from Brooklyn.
Unbeknownst to us the grandfather from St. Louis, Sam, told his son, Gary, that he thought he'd recognized my dad; they had served in WWII together. Gary was incredulous: "C'mon dad, you haven't seen him since V E Day. That's almost forty years ago. He's from New York; all Jews from New York look like that." Sam insisted that it was my dad just by the way he walked and by his mannerisms, so Gary reluctantly sent the guy who was

running our trip over to our table to ask my dad if he'd fought in the war and if he was with a specific unit.

With Sam and Gary standing at their table, they watched as my dad nodded yes to the questions and then they walked over.

It was incredible. Dad stood up and he and Sam fell into each other's arms.

When my dad was discharged he went back to Brooklyn and Sam went back to St. Louis. They'd had no contact in all that time.

We laughed and cried as everybody was introduced: Sam, his wife Ruth, Gary, and Gary's two children Greta and Jonathan, my dad Dave, my mom Lotte, and the three of us; Gary's wife had passed away a few years earlier.

Sam or my dad, the remembrance is a little muddy here, reached into his pocket, pulled out his wallet and extracted a picture of the two of them, in uniform, saluting a flagpole while in Europe. It was too much. People were moved, families jostled and the Mandel/Shanker families became one.

The next day, while eating lunch, a young boy walked by our table. I looked at him and asked his name (I never forget a face). With the cutest little voice he said: "Ryan Ennis."

"Are you related to Jay Ennis," I asked. This little kid had the exact same face as the Jay Ennis that I went to elementary school with and also hadn't seen since 1960.

"Yup," he said, "he's my daddy and he's right over there." What made this voice cuter was that his r's were said as w's. Jay, seeing that his five year old son was in conversation with strangers, strode over. It was my turn to stand up and give him a hug. He knew who I was the minute I introduced myself. Jay was there with his dad, dad's girlfriend, wife Susan and their three kids: Sean, Dara and Ryan.

That night, and for the rest of the trip, we were a table of seventeen.

We were close to twenty people in 1985 when we made arrangements to spend Pesach in The Bahamas together. We got down to the dining room for the first Seder and asked if we could set up outside at the pool. It was a glorious night. A huge moon with a gazillion stars lit up the sky and the hotel had burning torches lighting up the pool area around which we were sitting.

There was another family sitting nearby, six people that appeared to be a bubby, mom, dad and three kids. Our Seder was, is and G-D Willing will always be, fun, very loud with lots of singing.

Mel, the father at the other table, walked up and asked if his family might join our Seder. We moved their table into the middle of ours, put their kids next to our kids and continued long into the night. So now we were twenty seven: Mel and his wife Susan (another Susan), his mom Nellie ('bubby') and Cindy, Lowell and Jeffrey, their kids. Cindy and Greta were the same age, Lowell, Jonathan, Sean, Dara, Jeff and Wayne were within a year of each other and Ryan tagged along.

From Cross To Cross

    Over the course of the past twenty years we've been to many places together and we've celebrated and grieved together as a family, extended though it may be. As I said before, our children now have (or are about to have) children of their own, and although the family units are growing, we still try to maintain Pesach together.

    The Vanderbilt estate--money or the lack thereof--is what sent me on the Passover journey in my mind. In any case, we were in Asheville, it was still raining and we had the car, so the four of us drove around the rest of the day stopping at various points of interest and then headed back to the motel. Bobby and I wondered if our bikes would start after two days of torrential downpour; they did. Clifford, however, the stuffed dog that adorns Bob and Nedda's luggage rack, was sopping wet. Poor Clifford!

    When we got up the next morning we returned the car, got a ride back to the motel, and donned our rain gear--right, it was still raining. We had breakfast and headed out the back roads towards route 129 and Deal's Gap, Tennessee. We rode southwest; little did I know that the next section of the ride would be a history lesson about the Cherokee.

Chapter 18
Day Five Heading into Tennessee

I had never thought about the plight of the Indians in the eastern part of the United States: specifically the Cherokee.

The rain had subsided; it was a welcome change. Riding beautiful back roads on dry pavement and seeing the, now very green, foliage delighted us. As we rode along route 19 in North Carolina, heading towards Tennessee, there were billboards, the exact wording escapes me, that spoke of getting over the traumas of the past and looking towards a bright future. Shelly and I were puzzled at the first billboard, and quizzed each other as to the meaning after the second billboard; neither of us had a clue. As a matter of fact, we rode through the town of Cherokee and didn't even connect it with the nation.

There were lots of motels, and far in the distance there was a tall building that stood out from the Great Smokey Mountains. Why would anyone build up as opposed to out? I thought. There was land, land and more land; it was still 'open spaces' here.

We rode past the building and laughed: "Welcome to Harrah's Cherokee Casino & Hotel."

There's a story of a ventriloquist whose car broke down in the desert on his way to Las Vegas.
As he sat on the side of the road an Indian walking with a horse a dog and a sheep stopped to see if he could help.
The ventriloquist thought he'd have some fun so he asked the Indian if the horse spoke.
"Horse no talk," the Indian said.
With that the ventriloquist asked: "Hey, horse, how's it going?"
The ventriloquist, throwing his voice, answered as the horse: "Things are good. I'm an old horse, look at my swayback. I don't get ridden anymore and I spend the day grazing, drinking from a clear stream or sleeping."
The ventriloquist asked the Indian if the dog spoke.
"Dog no talk," the Indian said.
With that the ventriloquist asked: "Hey, dog, how's it going?"
The ventriloquist, throwing his voice answered as the dog:"Things are great. I'm an old dog, I hardly get kicked, people throw me scraps of food and old bones to chew on, but mostly I just lie around in the shade."
The Indian couldn't believe what he was hearing. The ventriloquist was having so much fun he turned and asked one more time. "Tell me," he asked," does your sheep speak."
The Indian looked at the sheep turned to the ventriloquist and said: "sheep lie, sheep lie."

It was later that day when we ran into a biker who told us about 'The Trail of Tears Commemorative Motorcycle Ride.'

    There was a small faction of Cherokee who, in 1835, signed a treaty ceding all of their tribal lands east of the Mississippi River to the federal government for five million dollars, and in return, the government was giving them new homes in what is now Oklahoma. Most of the Indians refused to abide by this fraudulently gotten treaty and wouldn't leave, so, in 1838, President Andrew Jackson ordered the Cherokee arrested and held prisoners in stockades until they could be moved.
    More than fifteen thousand people were marched, more than one thousand miles from their homes in Georgia, Tennessee and North Carolina, to their new homes. More than one thousand died on the way; hunger, disease and exhaustion were the major causes of their deaths.

    My heart went out to the people of the Cherokee nation. We've all suffered and we've all been marched into the unknown, into some form of living hell. We've all stood on 'that line'.

    One of the first times I ever heard Elie Wiesel speak, he was talking about his childhood in Romania. He was from the town of Sighet, a town which no longer exists: well, at least not for Jews. He related the story of the day the Nazis came into town, and I won't quote him because it would be misquoting him.
    They lined some of the Jews up, left them standing on this line until they were ready to march the Jews out of

town. The line passed right by his house. Elie and his sisters were out in the yard, the Jews on the line were begging for water, and Elie and his sisters ran into the house and brought them whatever they could carry.
As Elie spoke he said: "two days later we were on that line and I'm still on that line today."

It was one of the most powerful statements I'd ever heard and the more I thought about it the more I cried. That's right, I thought, every one of us is still on some line and you guys never let us off.
It's tough to ride with tears in your eyes but this image, the image that Elie Wiesel left with me, the image of a normal life turned into HELL, is still burned deep into my being.

I add a passage from Elie Wiesel's book Night, one of the most powerful passages in all of literature, Holocaust literature for sure, and may represent the feelings of many, but certainly the experience of every Jew who lived in the camps.
"Never shall I forget that night, the first night in camp, which has turned my life into one long night, seven times cursed and seven times sealed. Never shall I forget that smoke. Never shall I forget the little faces of the children, whose bodies I saw turned into wreaths of smoke beneath a silent blue sky.
Never shall I forget those flames which consumed my faith forever.
Never shall I forget that nocturnal silence which deprived me, for all eternity, of the desire to live. Never shall I forget those moments which murdered my God and my soul and turned my dreams to dust. Never shall I

forget these things, even if I am condemned to live as long as God Himself. Never."

"...to remain silent and indifferent is the greatest sin of all...," this is, in a terse way, Elie Wiesel's view on life.

I wrote earlier about the play Two. In that play, Rabbi Levy explains to Anna why he became an atheist. He says, "... I knew a boy once who had both limbs removed yet he could still feel his toes wriggling, still feel a pain in his calf or an itch in his foot. Well, three years ago my G-D was removed..."

This is fiction, conceptually true for many Jews but fiction nonetheless. Elie Wiesel's G-D was removed but his story is not fiction, his fiction is truth, his fiction is reality. He lived through it, and, he is still on that line today.

Getting back to The Cherokee Nation, I actually have a theory about the Indians. They could be the lost tribe of Israel.

Ay yay yay yay, Ay yay yay yay, Ay yay yay yay, Ay yay yay.

You may or may not know this, but I think that it's all about the music. You know how I feel about the rhythms of the prayers, and how I believe that takes you to a higher level.

Here's a theory of mine, which after reading, many of you will either be convinced that I have no grasp on reality, or that I'm just making this up as I go along. Jacob had twelve sons, from which come the twelve tribes of Israel. Joseph, Jacob's eleventh son, had two sons, Ephraim and Menasheh, who split up his inheritance, adding a thirteenth tribe.

Lenny Mandel

In about 1988 there was a play on Broadway called Chu-Chem, pronounced choo-chem. It was about the lost tribe of Israel who, in their wanderings, ended up in China. It wasn't CHOO as in choo choo, it was ch as pronounced in Hebrew or Yiddish, chu-chem, and meant smart (the first of the four sons in the Haggadah is the Chacham–the wise son). The idiom in Yiddish means simpleton. So, if you were to call someone a chuchem, you're calling him an idiot.

Nobody has been able to figure out what happened to that thirteenth tribe, so China could've been as good a possibility as any. Interesting assumption, no?

Let's assume that this 'lost tribe' made it to China, stayed for a while and moved on. Where would they go? Certainly not back from whence they came, no, they'd go to the East, of course. They crossed the Bering Sea, the Bering Strait, went into Alaska (much too cold for our ancestors), down through Canada, ending up across the border into North America (now The United States).

A few weeks ago I was at a Hasidic Bar Mitzvah celebration; I was the only person wearing a ponytail in the back of my head. Don't get me wrong, everyone there had a ponytail, but they wore them in ringlets alongside their ears. Strange place to wear your ponytail, I thought, as I watched them dance.

Ay yay yay yay, Ay yay yay yay, Ay yay yay yay, Ay yay yay. Around in a large circle, each man with his hand on the shoulder of the man in front of him, all the men dancing together. Their left legs moved into the circle, all in unison, and then another small step again with the left. Their right legs, next, moved to the outside with another small step immediately following. One large undulating sea of men, and the rhythm; Ay yay yay yay, Ay yay yay yay, Ay yay yay yay, Ay yay yay.

    In my mind I went back to the hundreds of cowboy movies I watched growing up. Then I thought of The Frisco Kid where Gene Wilder played a Hasidic Rabbi from Poland on his way to San Francisco who, among other misfortunes, gets captured by Indians. Picture them dancing. C'mon think about it. Hear their rhythms:Ay yay yay yay, Ay yay yay yay, Ay yay yay yay, Ay yay yay.
    I know that you can both hear and see it. You can see them dance, all men, around a huge fire, the chanting elevating them to great heights. Where did they come from? Doesn't their dancing and chanting sound like ours?
    How about this: they, the American Indians, are the descendants of the lost tribe of Israel. They fled from country to country finally settling down where, it appeared, they'd be left alone. Left to worship any way they pleased, in peace.
    So wadda-u-think? Lenny is crazy? We know that without you.
    So wadda-u-think? Lenny is pulling your leg? He's been known to do that on occasion.
    So wadda-u-think? Lenny should stick to music and leave history, even the history he invents, to historians?
    C'mon, wadda-u-think?

    I doubt that there is a people, a nation, a country, a race or religion that hasn't felt that pain, that hasn't been removed from a former life to face the unknown. Myriad cultures were belittled, treated as if they were lower than animals, starved, tortured and killed: and none more than the Jews.

> *Five men walked into a bar in Buenos Aires, Argentina, sat down at a table and asked the bartender for five beers.*
> *"I know you," the bartender said, "I definitely know you."*
> *The men were adamant that he would have no possibility of knowing them since they'd never been in that bar before, but after a few minutes of back and forth banter one man said: "Alright, you know me, I'm Adolph Hitler."*
> *"Hitler," he queried, "but we thought you were dead!"*
> *"Everybody thinks I am dead," he replied, "but I'm not. We're here building a bomb."*
> *"A bomb?" he asked.*
> *"Yes, this time we're going to kill seven million Jews and five acrobats," Hitler replied.*
> *"Five acrobats," he said incredulously," why are you going to kill five acrobats?"*
> *Hitler turned to his friends and said: "I told you, nobody cares about the Jews!"*

"...Ridi Paglaicco..." so goes the Aria Vesti La Giubba from Leoncavallo's Pagliacci. The clown who is always laughing on the outside while his heart breaks on the inside.

Yes, the Jews and their tears; tears for themselves and despite the teachings of the racists, for others as well. Where would the civil rights movement be without the

Jews? I'd laugh if it didn't piss me off the way we are portrayed regarding the blacks. Right, I said blacks.

    This whole new thing about being a whatever-you-are/American is crap. African/Americans, Irish/Americans, Greek/Americans, get over it. You are Americans, and prefacing that fact is divisive. What am I, a Jewish/American? Hell, I was born here and I have an American passport. Oh, I guess that makes me an American/American—how novel.
    I know that every race, every nationality went through, if not one, then many tortuous times. What I never understood, and still don't, is when people ask what you are, you answer what your nationality is. I'm Italian, I'm Polish, I'm a Scot etc they say, and you, you are a Jew. Is that my nationality all of a sudden, or have I always been an outcast everywhere I went? That haunts me.
    I've always been proud to be an American even during my hippie years when I questioned everything our government did.

    I read a story, first excerpted in Hadassah Magazine, about Jewish soldiers in the U.S. Army who were being sent to the Middle-East to fight in the first Iraqi war. They were told that their dog tags were to be stamped "Protestant B," a coded designation for the Jewish religion. [I expect that was for their protection in case of being captured?] "Protestant B, Not" is about the experience of Retired Army Major Mike Neulander and is excerpted from the book This Jewish Life: Stories of Discovery, Connection and Joy by Debra B.Darvick. "Protestant B., Not" is based on an interview

Lenny Mandel

Ms. Darvick conducted with Mike Neulander who now lives in Newport News, Virginia.

Dog tags. When you get right down to it, the military's dog tag classification forced me to reclaim my Judaism. In the fall of 1990, things were heating up in Kuwait and Saudi Arabia. I had been an Army Captain and a helicopter maintenance test pilot for a decade and received notice that I would be transferred to the First Cavalry Division[,] which was on alert for the Persian Gulf War. Consequently, I also got wind of the Department of Defense "dog tag dilemma" vis-□-vis Jewish personnel.

Then, as now, Jews were forbidden by Saudi law to enter the country. But our Secretary of Defense flat out told the King of Saudi Arabia, "We have Jews in our military.

They've trained with their units and they're going. Blink and look the other way." With Kuwait occupied and the Iraqis at his border, King Faud did the practical thing. We shipped out, but there was still the issue of the dog tag classification.

Normally the dog tags of Jewish servicemen are imprinted with the word "Jewish." But our Department of Defense, fearing that maintaining this customary marking for Jewish soldiers would put them at further risk should they be captured on Iraqi soil, substituted the classification, "Protestant B," on the tags, "B" being a secret code for Jew. I didn't like the whole idea of classifying Jews as Protestant anything and so I decided to leave my dog tag alone. I figured if I were captured, it was in God's hands.

Changing my tags was tantamount to denying my religion, and I couldn't swallow that. In September, 1990 I went off to defend a country that I was prohibited from entering. The "Jewish" classification on my dog tag remained, clear and unmistakable as the American star pinned on the hood of every Army truck.

A few days after my arrival, the Baptist chaplain approached me. "I just got a secret message through channels," he said. There's going to be a Jewish gathering. A holiday? Simkatoro or something like that. You want to go? It's at 1800 hours at Dhahran Airbase."

"Simkatoro" turned out to be Simchas Torah, a holiday that hadn't registered on my religious radar in eons. But registered then and there. Services were held in absolute secrecy in a windowless room in a cinder-block building in Dhahran, Saudi Arabia. Rabbi Romer, the chaplain who helped keep us together during the war, led a swift and simple service. We couldn't risk singing or dancing, but Rabbi Ben Romer had managed to smuggle in a bottle of Manischewitz.

Normally, I can't stand the stuff, but that night, the wine tasted of Shabbes and family and Seders of long ago. My soul was warmed by the forbidden alcohol and by the memories swirling around me and my fellow soldiers. We were strangers to one another in a land stranger than any of us had ever experienced, but for that brief hour, we were home.

Only Americans would have had the chutzpah to celebrate Simchas Torah under the noses of the Saudis. Irony and pride twisted together inside me like barbed wire. Celebrating my Judaism that evening made me even prouder to be an American, made me thankful once more for the freedoms we have in this country. I'd only been in Saudi Arabia a week, but I already had a keen understanding of how restrictive Saudi society was.

Soon after that service, things began coming to a head; the next time I was able to do anything remotely Jewish was Chanukah. Maybe it was coincidence, or maybe it was God's hand that placed a Jewish Colonel in charge of our division's intelligence unit. Colonel Schneider's presence enabled him to get messages of Jewish gatherings to us immediately. Had a non-Jew been in that position, the information likely would have taken a back seat to a more pressing issue. Like war. But it didn't. When notice of the Chanukah party was decoded, we knew about it at once.

The first thing we saw when we entered the tent was food, seemingly tons of it. Care packages from the States: cookies, latkes, sour cream and applesauce, and for some funny reason, cans and cans of gefilte fish. The wind was blowing dry across the tent, but inside there was this incredible feeling of celebration. As Rabbi Romer talked about the theme of Chanukah and the ragtag bunch of Maccabee soldiers fighting Jewry's oppressors thousands of years ago, it wasn't hard to make the connection to what lay ahead of us. There in the middle of the desert, inside an olive green tent, we felt like we were the Maccabees ourselves. If we had to go down, we were going to go down fighting.

We blessed the candles, acknowledging the King of the Universe who commanded us to kindle the Chanukah lights.

We said the second prayer, praising God for the miracles He performed, bayamim hahem bazman hazeh, "in those days and now." And since we were assembled on the first night of Chanukah, we also sang the third blessing, the Sheheyanu, thanking God for keeping us in life and for enabling us to reach this season.

From Cross To Cross

We knew war was imminent. All week, we'd received reports of mass destruction, projections of the chemical weapons likely to be unleashed. Intelligence estimates put the first rounds of casualties at 12,500 soldiers. I heard those numbers and thought, "That's my entire division!"

I sat back in my chair, my three cans of gefilte fish at my feet. I had tucked a trio of letters addressed to "Any Jewish Soldier" into my back pocket. There we were in the desert, about to go to war, singing songs of praise to God who had saved our ancestors in battle. The feeling of unity was as pervasive as our apprehension, as real as the sand that found its way into everything from our socks to our toothbrushes.

I felt more Jewish there on that lonely Saudi plain, our tanks and guns at the ready, than I'd ever felt outfitted with tallis, prayer book, and yarmulke in shul.

That Chanukah in the desert solidified for me the urge to reconnect with my Judaism. I felt religion welling up inside me. Any soldier will tell you that there are no atheists in a foxhole, and I know a good deal of my feelings were tied to the looming war and my desire to get right with God before the unknown descended in the cloud of battle. It sounds corny, but as we downed the latkes and cookies and wiped the last of the apple sauce from our plates, everyone grew quiet, keenly aware of the link with history, thinking of what we were about to do and what had been done by soldiers like us so long ago.

The trooper beside me stared ahead at nothing in particular, absent-mindedly fingering his dog tag. "How'd you classify?" I asked, nodding to my tag.

Silently, he withdrew the metal rectangle and its

beaded chain from beneath his shirt and held it out for me to read. Like mine, his read, "Jewish."
Somewhere in a military depot someplace, I'm sure that there must be boxes and boxes of dog tags, still in their wrappers, all marked "Protestant B."

    Here are men of courage, I thought. Men who would stand up for their beliefs no matter if it would put them in harm's way.

    Our ride that morning, the ride through Cherokee, followed route 19 through gorgeous mountains, lush valleys and meadows. We didn't hear the footsteps of the marched Cherokee, we didn't hear the footsteps of the marched Jews--well, in our heads we certainly did--all we heard was the ever present whirring of our tires on the pavement.
    We were getting hungry and it was just about time for lunch so we stopped. We were in the town of Nantahala, North Carolina, and there was a neat looking place there, right on the Nantahala River.

Chapter 19
Same Day- mid afternoon—
Heading to Deals Gap

The hostess sat us at a table which made it seem like we were on a boat, cruising down the Nantahala River. We overlooked the rapids and watched kayaks and rafts run these waters; it seemed as if we were moving and the water stood still. It was a little weird for a while but after a few minutes we got used to it. I asked the waitress how many salt shakers were lost to the river, as we were sitting at the edge. She told us that there were very few of those lost, but plenty of bottles of ketchup.

We ate watching the flow of the water and I felt a little like Hesse's Siddartha finally sitting on the riverbank, understanding. Understanding what? I thought. Everything is still a great mystery. I wondered how a Shul would flourish in this very touristy area, laughed aloud and then thought about those three churches in Virginia: one hundred yards, three churches and very few people within thirty miles of those churches. The rain stopped and although clouds still covered the sky we packed our rain gear (albeit near the top of our saddlebags) and rode on.

Three miles later we were at the junction of route 129, Deals Gap: one of the reasons for taking this trip in the first place. Bob had never ridden Deal's Gap, an eleven mile stretch of route 129 with 318 turns, and wanted to, so that was our primary goal.

Bobby and I both love riding back roads, and route 129 is one of the best. It runs through gorgeous forests, up and down mountains, has some, more than interesting, turns, and we ride them more like the hare and never like the tortoise. Bob owns a Yamaha sport bike that he takes on the racetrack and I did the same with a BMW sport bike.

I remember when I was looking to buy a quick, lightweight motorcycle, specifically for twisty back road riding, and decided to demo a few different bikes up at Americade; the bike I was most interested in was a Triumph Speed Triple.

Americade is the touring motorcyclist's F.A.O. Schwartz. Not only can you see all the latest equipment, get technical advice from everyone about everything and get your bike painted or pinstriped, you can get the latest coffee mug holder that swings on a bezel (while attached to your ape-hangers) so that you can ride without spilling a drop. You can buy a new seat, fill your old one with gel-- for more comfort--add a sound system or buy new tires and there is more leather there than on the animals that still roam the Veldt. Americade's mall has the latest in 'biker-everything'.

There are nightly events planned: bike shows, light shows, rodeos and cruises on the lake but most of the attention nightly is paid to the bikes that are ridden or parked along the curb. I'm talking about more than sixty thousand motorcycles. They run the gamut from antiques to radicals to stockers to designs that are so outrageous you wouldn't believe them if I included pictures. It's an event to just hang out and meet wonderful people, or ride some magnificent back roads and mountain trails. There are plenty of interesting places to see, many of which aren't mentioned in the local guidebooks.

It was late in the day and most of the demo rides were over as we headed over to the Triumph exhibit. The Triumph Speed Triple was the bike that I was very anxious to demo, but because of the late hour I was sure that I'd missed my chance.

I got there to find that Rob Tonnesen, an old friend, was one of the guides on the Triumph demos. He told me that if I waited, I could ride with him to scout new trails for the next day's rides after the day's demos were over. I was ecstatic. Rob told us that there would be six of us riding: Rob, another guide, two of 'Team-Triumph's' finest and the two of us.

Let me tell you about the guys from 'Team Triumph'. They were about twenty seven maybe twenty eight years old with forty six inch shoulders and thirty inch waists. They were wearing skin tight leather pants, jackets sporting the Triumph logo and, of course, full-face helmets. Now me, I've got a fifty inch chest but a thirty eight inch waist, and I'm wearing jeans, sneakers, a denim jacket, sunglasses and a brain bucket. I didn't care, I threw my leg over the 509 Speed Triple; I was ready to ride.

The back roads upstate New York are gorgeous, and while looking around I realized that the boys up front were nowhere in sight so I tweaked the throttle; the speed limit sign read 35 mph but my speedo read 65. The trees whizzed by, the rush of the wind was even louder now but I still couldn't see the boys. Unbeknownst to me, the three guys who are trailing me had lost sight of me as well. I never looked behind me.

This type of riding is wonderful, it's fast, it's smooth and because the Speed Triple is so light, it is much easier to toss around than my FL; what a delightful change. I rode another five minutes or so until I came around a bend and there they were, sitting on their bikes, waiting for the rest of us to catch up.

We hung out for a bit, a couple of us swapped bikes and we were off again. No hanging back anymore, we were a pack of six swarming motorcycles out on a tear. We rode back road curves, sweeping and acute, long and some not so long straight-aways, at exhilarating speeds.

The TT boys were in front of us and it was awesome watching them setting up for turns, diving into them and emerging. They were in a rhythm and I tried to emulate them, albeit at a slower pace. We turned right and flew over a bridge, then left as the road curved, a beautiful sweeping curve, which led us up a hill.

It looked as if the hill went on forever, and I, now directly behind the boys, twisted my throttle to catch them. They twisted at the same time, but the 509 was no match for the 595s they were riding. The hill crested into a long straightaway and we were roaring, until we ran out of paved road. Yup, we went from blacktop to gravel and never saw it coming. The bike slows down very quickly when you release the throttle and down shift, like a son of a gun; luckily no one went down.

It was time to turn around and head back. We knew exactly what to expect for a couple of miles so the TT boys took off, side by side, down the straightaway and into the descending hill with the rest of us on their heels, throttles wide open.

So, there I was riding a bike, smallish in size for a man of my bulk, with no crash bars--I thought to myself, in a semi upright, semi bent over the tank position. My brain bucket, which was strapped as tight as possible to my head, was tap dancing on my skull anyway, and my face felt like I was in a five-G dive in an F-16 fighter. I must've looked like a Sharpei (the dog with all the wrinkles) on the run.

My right hand had the throttle open and opening wider, and as I glanced at the Speedometer, the needle was pegged dead center (you don't even want to know what the numbers dead center on that speedometer were) and moving to the right. I can't remember now whether I just released the throttle or told myself that I was completely out of my mind before I let go. It doesn't matter; it was very fast, getting faster, and I was out of my league. These guys had tons of experience on these bikes, and although I ride my FL like a sport bike on the back roads at speed, this was a new experience. We ended up on the highway and the six of us were doing one hundred plus mph in a perfect stagger, coming around another sweeping curve.

Back at the demo center and off the bikes, every inch of exposed skin on my body was tingling, and my face hurt, but not from pain. We couldn't stop thanking them, and I couldn't help thinking that I had to get a Triumph. Well, I got my Triumph, but it was a 1970 Bonneville chopper. Ah yes, my face pain, well, that was from the huge grin that was plastered on it the entire ride.

Just outside of Nantahala, we rode through the Joyce Kilmer Memorial Forest. When I was young I thought that Joyce Kilmer was a woman. There was a small triangle on Kings Highway and East 12th Street in Brooklyn that was named for Joyce Kilmer and until I saw an old James Cagney film, The Fighting 69th, I had no idea who he was; by the time I got to High School I was familiar with his work.

High school was my departure from the 'Jewish' world into the secular. I didn't hate Yeshiva but I didn't love it either.

These are two of my favorite stories from my years of growing up in the 'Jewish' world.
I was about eight or nine and I was going trick or treating. I know it sounds weird for a Yeshiva boy to be celebrating this pagan ritual, but to me it wasn't a holiday or a ritual, and I wasn't celebrating it. This was all of my friends running around the neighborhood dressed in costumes, getting tons of candy.
So, it was a Thursday night and I was going from door to door in my apartment building of eighty four families, ringing bells and saying: "trick or treat!"

From Cross To Cross

When I got to the Fisch's apartment Mrs. Fisch opened the door, looked at me incredulously and said: "what are you doing here, Lenny, Halloween is tomorrow night."

"I know, Mrs. Fisch," I replied, "but tomorrow night is Shabbes and I can't go trick or treating on Shabbes." The whole apartment building laughed for years at that story.

I laughed out loud as we rode along.

Tommy was one of eight siblings, I can't remember his last name, but his folks were from the other side of the pond and both spoke with a brogue so heavy that I could hardly understand them.

We were hanging out on his stoop on East 17th Street and he asked me to take over for one of the altar boys at St. Brendan's on Sunday. He said it would be easy-- all I'd have to do was stand there with either my hands folded, or outstretched with palms up. At least that's the way I remember it.

I laughed: "so what am I gonna say after mass when the Priest comes up to me, tells me that I don't look familiar and asks what parish my family belongs to: Young Israel of Flatbush," I asked? I wouldn't have had the balls to do it anyway, but I'd have thought about it.

It was great being friends with all these kids but behind closed doors, who knows what was really said. The kids my age never fought with me and never called me names--hey, I was better off than Rudolph.

The older kids were a totally different story; Mockie and Kike were their favorites with an occasional Jew bastard thrown in. I really don't care what happened to the older kids and although I'd love to know where some of the kids I used to play with are--it's been a very long time.

After elementary school, my parents gave me three high schools to choose from: Yeshiva Torah V'Da'at, The Mirer Yeshiva or The Brooklyn Talmudic Academy. All three were ultra-Orthodox schools. I told my folks that I'd applied to Stuyvesant High School, had already taken the entrance exam, and that if I got accepted that was where I wanted to go. Neither of my parents had any idea what Stuyvesant High School was, but my dad nodded and said, "Yeah, yeah, Stuyvesant High School, we'll see."

For those of you not familiar with the New York City public schools, Stuyvesant High School was, and probably still is, the number one public high school in America (I know the Bronx High School of Science grads will have something to say about that statement—wrong though they be). The poet Ogden Nash wrote a poem that I think should be on every T-shirt at Stuyvesant. I have to paraphrase it, but it sort of says The Bronx, no thanks.

Needless to say I was accepted, informed my parents, and waited for the isolation booth. It was my father's method of letting you know that he was very upset and wanted to talk to you. We'd go into whichever room was unoccupied and I'd always come out with tears streaming down my face.

I remember when Phillip Goldberg, one of my two 'best friends' growing up came home, on leave, from the Army. He was stationed at Fort Bliss, in El Paso, Texas and had taken up skydiving. At dinner Phil began talking about taking me skydiving with him. He was sure that I'd love it. Before he even got a chance to finish his sentence my dad summoned him into the isolation booth. Needless to say Phil had completely changed his mind about my jumping out of a plane when they got back to the table. I don't know that he ever jumped again.

As I got older, when my father asked me into the isolation booth I would say, "Hit me, dad, please, it's much less painful."

"I should've forced you to go to Yeshiva. That Stuyvesant High School was your ruination," was what my mother used to say: words that she reiterates to this day. I went anyway.

It was a forty five minute subway ride to school in Manhattan, and my first day was in September of 1960 when hurricane Dana hit New York City. The subways were all diverted and I found myself 20 minutes from home in Coney Island, where I was put on a bus and driven up Coney Island Avenue to Avenue N; I was about seven blocks from home.

The wind was incredible and the rain that pelted me stung like a million sharp needles.

> *A man crossing East 14th Street on Avenue N got hit by a tree, and while lying on the ground bleeding, he screamed for a priest. St. Brendan's was two blocks away and Father O'Brien came to administer last rites.*

> *Kneeling over the man Father O'Brien asked his name.*
> *"Abe Cohen", he replied.*
> *"Abe Cohen," the Priest answered? "You need a Rabbi not a Priest."*
> *Cohen replied, "Are you kidding, call a Rabbi out in this weather?"*

Actually, hurricane Dana really did hit us on my first day of high school. Abe Cohen and the Priest? What can I tell you?

The kids in my class were from all over the city and of every race, religion and nationality. It was an incredible first few weeks for me. There were plenty of Jewish kids. As a matter of fact, the majority of the kids at Stuyvesant were Jewish; that's not true any longer. We nicknamed it The Little Yeshiva, or, to piss off my religious relatives who kept hocking me about going to a Yeshiva high school, I'd tell them I was going to St. Uyvesant. I thought it was pretty funny.

Stuyvesant High School was a real eye opener for me; talk about a melting pot. Marty Paull and Matt Proujansky were Jewish. Mike Coughlin, Johnny Capello, Al Angiola, were Irish or Italian and Catholic. Phil Jones, Rudy Scott and Tom Shick were black. Bohdan Turynskyj, Myron Yasiejko and Steve Rudyk were all Ukranian Catholic, and came from St. Georges parochial school. Bart Inkeles, Syd Leinwand and Dave Bednarsh were three kids from an orthodox Yeshiva on the lower east side, and the list, if I were to continue, would go on and on.

From Cross To Cross

As I walked up the stairs one day, an upper classman ran by me, pulled the sweater that was draped over my shoulders off, and threw it on the ground. I ran after him calling him all kinds of names. At that point he turned around and, with three guys standing next to him, started down the stairs toward me. I didn't blink and I felt a hand on my shoulder: "Fuck 'em, let 'em come." I turned around. Johnny Capello, Phil Jones and Mike Coughlin were standing right beside me and the four of us made a move, as one, at the seniors. They split pretty quickly. We stood there on the landing between floors smacking each other on the back, reveling in our triumph. It was a strong bond that was only broken after graduation as we all went our separate ways.

I was perplexed. Where were my Jewish classmates? They were walking up the stairs with me but when the confrontation started they were nowhere to be seen. My whole life I was led to believe that Jews stick together and that we never let one another down. This was a learning experience for me and over time I stopped wondering about it.

My life was changing as I grew in this new environment and I began a departure, a slow but sure departure, from my life as a semi-observant Jew to that of a secular Jew. Shabbes evening I was still with my family but as soon as dinner was over I was gone. Folk singing clubs in 'The Village' or just hanging out with my new friends. I never stayed home. I decided to really become an American kid and tried out for the football team; in high school, football is played on Shabbes in New York City.

Lenny Mandel

Mark Kiel tells the story of a boy who comes home after his first semester in college.

> *"Pop," he says, "I just studied Philosophy 101, Sociology 101, Anthropology 101 and Psychology 101, and I don't believe in G-D anymore."*
> *His father shrugged his shoulders, they finished dinner and the boy went out.*
> *Eight thirty the next morning the boy is woken up by his father: "Wake up, it's time to go to Shul."*
> *"What are you doing?" he asked," I told you I just studied Philosophy 101, Sociology 101, Anthropology 101 and Psychology 101, and I don't believe in G-D anymore."*
> *"G-D, shmod," replied the father,"Shabbes we go to Shul."*

I wasn't very good at football; I thought that I'd walk onto the field and be able to play. Exercise? Run laps? You've got to be kidding. It didn't last very long.

Riding these beautiful back roads heading to Deal's Gap from Nantahala there weren't a lot of churches, but there were plenty of crosses. They were either singles, doubles or in threes. The three Crosses sent my thoughts back to Barcelona, Spain where I'd spent a couple of years when I was in my early twenties.

CHAPTER 20
BARCELONA 1969 in my MIND

Barcelona is one of the most beautiful cities in the world, and one of my favorites. The city lies nestled between two mountains--Tibidabo and Montjuich; Montjuich, the mountain of the Jews.

During the Spanish Inquisition, not only were Jews not allowed to practice Judaism, they were forced to convert to Catholicism or they were burned at the stake. The people of Catalonia were a wonderfully benevolent society and allowed their Jews (one of my favorite expressions--their Jews) to work during the day and retire at night up on the mountain. As a buddy of mine said as we walked the mountaintop, "Can you imagine the tears that were shed on this hill?"

I'm not really sure about the benevolence of the Catalan people, but I am of their savvy. The Jews ran the businesses in Barcelona, and they did most of the trade. The Catalan people realized that without the Jews their economy would suffer, so the Prince of Catalonia made that decree.

Why are Jews always involved in trade, in business? Easy, it wasn't until the last few hundred years that they were allowed to go to school and become professionals; they never had a choice. As a matter of

Lenny Mandel

fact, until 1964 you couldn't matriculate and go on to university in Spain if you weren't Catholic.

I occasionally worked at Radio Nacional de Espana when I lived in Barcelona. It wasn't exactly work; I was a disc jockey, well, sort of. During the broadcasts kids would sit along the walls of the studio and I, a set of earphones on my head and a microphone at my mouth, sat at the DJ's table. I was 'Lenny.' Yes, I know I am Lenny but that was my radio persona both over the airwaves and in the studio. One of the kids who hung out at the studio showed me a greeting card. It was in Spanish, with a picture of the Madonna on it; I had no idea what I was looking at. Constantino (it was his show that I was 'guest hosting' or being the guest DJ on--he was the number one DJ in Spain and a very close friend) turned to him and said: "He has no idea what you are showing him, he is a Jew;" the sentence was, of course, in Spanish, as was the word for Jew: Judeo.
This kid, stunned, looked at me and said: "Judeo? Judeo? Judeo? Lenny, Judeo...?" This went on for what seemed like forever and I turned, touched the sides of my head and said: "Lo siento, mi cuernos estan abajo ahora (I'm sorry; my horns are down right now)." He was devastated. How could someone he looked up to, someone that he respected and liked, be a Jew? I turned on my heel and walked out.

Constantino explained that this kid had probably never seen a Jew in his life, or if he had he wouldn't know it. His upbringing, as that of ninety five percent of all Spaniards, was strictly Catholic. Constantino quipped that

From Cross To Cross

when the pope died they mourned for three days in Rome but for seven days in Spain.

    I watched a girl dancing at a disco in Barcelona one night, wearing a rather large Magen David around her neck. I asked her if she were Jewish and when she replied in the affirmative I asked if they forced her to wear that star.
    "NO," she replied emphatically; she wore it because she was proud of it.
    I was bursting with pride and then a quick dose of fear came over me. We had a drink, we had a dance and I left the club feeling wonderful and safe.
    Aaah, safe, the magic word; we'll see.

    Back to the three Crosses which led my thoughts to Barcelona. The first time I'd ever seen three crosses together was in Barcelona. They, however, were nothing like the ones in Pennsylvania, Virginia, North Carolina, Tennessee, Kentucky and West Virginia; not even close. The three crosses in Barcelona are in the middle of Parc Guell, what we called Gaudi Park--named for the architect whose work adorns it: Anton Gaudi. He is perhaps the most famous architect in Spanish history.
    From the candy-like spires at the Park's mouth to the mystical tunnels, to the various shapes flowing with style and color, his work is incredible. Lizards, staircases, the undulating ceilings in his tunnels, the concrete park bench rippling as if it were a ribbon along the Park's edge, each and every one was intricately created with tiny mosaic tiles. You walk through the Parc until you get to his sculpture of the three crosses.

Gaudi's three Crosses stand atop a mountain of rocks, in the middle of the park, and you must climb the outer rim of these rocks to reach the top. It's not very high; you couldn't have said that about us back then!
These crosses are made up of one very tall cross facing you and the other two much smaller crosses, flanking the center cross, facing the sides. One resembles a T-square as the top of the cross appears as if covered; it is, but was created so. The three are dedicated, but not to 'Father, Son nor Holy Spirit,' nope. The tall cross is dedicated to the sun, the smaller to the moon, and the covered cross to total darkness.

Interesting concepts for a turn of the century Catholic, and we spent many days and nights up there discussing it. We came to the conclusion that the Mescaline back then must have been fabulous, and judging by most of his work, we felt that hallucinogenic drugs played a large part in his life. Hey, it's a theory.

Don't think I didn't ride motorcycles while I was in Spain, I did; Frank and Andy, two friends of mine from Brooklyn and the guys that wrote the song that begins this book, and I decided to rent motorcycles and take a few days ride down the coast. We each took a sleeping bag in which we rolled a change of clothes in case of rain. Frank strapped his guitar to the passenger seat, and off we rode. We headed west toward Sitges, a town down the coast.

What a gorgeous ride it is along the Mediterranean Sea. I was singing I Can See For Miles by the Who and

From Cross To Cross

On The Road Again by Canned Heat, and Andy joined in as we rode side by side.

The road started to rise along the cliffs, and as we looked to our left we could see the sea getting farther and farther below us. We wanted to stop and marvel at the sight spread out below, but the road began to twist and turn and the trucks never stopped coming. We held on at times, knuckles blazing white, wondering whether the joy was worth the risk. It was, and we continued, albeit singing with a bit less volume, until the road descended to sea level.

We'd begun this trip in mid-afternoon, and now the sun was beginning to set; we decided to find a place to camp for the night.

After a few minutes of searching the area, we came upon a beautiful clearing in the woods, parked the bikes and started making camp. We dug a small pit where our fire would be, and while Frank gathered wood, hopefully enough to maintain a fire through the night, Andy and I rode into town for food. We were no longer in Barcelona, but in a tiny village. There were no Supermarkets here and no one spoke English, which made it an interesting marketing experience as neither Andy nor I spoke very much Spanish.

Let's see: plenty of beer, potato chips, eggs, potatoes, rolls, cake, chocolate spread (it's like peanut butter, only chocolate), cheese and salami; a veritable banquet, to be sure. They gave us a large cardboard box, helped secure it, and therefore our groceries to my bike, and waved goodbye.

It was dark and the fire glowed as we sat around singing, all the while marveling at the sky above us and our beautiful surroundings. A twig snapped in the woods, and as the three of us turned toward the sound we were surrounded.

I don't remember there being more than six or seven of them, and the strains of Dueling Banjos (which wasn't even published until 1972) echoed through the forest. Not only the hair on the back of my neck, but the hair on the hair on the back of my neck stood at attention.

"Ola", they said.

"Ola", we replied in unison.

They sat down and we offered them our food and something to drink. It is considered impolite to refuse, so they accepted and we all sat around drinking, eating and attempting conversation. Frank started playing some Spanish tunes, and we sang along or played impromptu drums.

We had long finished our beer and most of the food we'd bought. Lo and behold three or four more men, wheeling a cart behind them, showed up. They unloaded cases of beer, fruit, cakes and a couple of their own instruments. They tossed me one of the bottles of beer that they'd brought. Alas, there was no way of drinking, as we didn't have an opener. "No te preoccupies," they said (don't worry) as they tossed the bottle to one of the guys who, with a huge grin on his face, opened it with his teeth.

We were up pretty much all night singing, drinking, talking, eating and laughing until they realized that their workday was beginning. So, with wonderful hugs and a huge adios, they left. We got an hour or two of sleep after they'd gone, and rode back to Barcelona the next day. It's been thirty years since that adventure, and the most vivid picture still in my mind is of the gleam of our fire off of the front teeth of the man who smiled as he opened my beer bottle. His teeth, you see, were gold.

Actually, I got my first Harley in Barcelona. A Brit named Johnny loaned the bike to me but he never came back. It was a 1946 Harley Davidson flathead with a tank shift and a suicide clutch. The suicide clutch might be a bit much to explain, but the tank shift is exactly that: a shifter which is not controlled by your foot. Rather it is a stick shift mounted on the gas tank and used as a stick shift on a car would be--with your hand.
The bike was bigger than most of the cars on the road there; most Spaniards drove Seats (pronounced say-aaht), Spanish Fiats, and believe me, they were small. I rode that bike all over Catalonia and everyone knew it and, by default, me as well. It was a trip and, as I was, sort of, a celebrity there anyway it just added to the attraction.

Safety, I wonder if many Jews really consider themselves safe? Maybe that's the problem, knowing what we know and re-living past insanities, we only feel safe, truly safe among our own kind and in our own milieu. We are city folk, having left the rural life in Poland and Russia generations ago.
I rarely think about how vulnerable we are sitting out here on a motorcycle at eighty plus miles an hour. I do, however, think about how vulnerable I am away from my 'safety net', my home, my friends and my people.

Chapter 21
Still Heading to Deals Gap, Thinking About My Dad

It's nearly impossible for me to ride my motorcycle without thinking of my dad. I still have a picture of him standing with his motorcycle in Vienna just days before Hitler marched in. He was a tough son of a bitch and I miss him. This story pretty much sums it up.

There I stood, up on the Bimah Friday night October 25th. The corresponding Hebrew calendar date was the 19th of Cheshvan. How interesting, I thought. My dad died on the 25th of October in 1994 and the Hebrew calendar date was the 20th of Cheshvan. Friday night, erev Shabbat, I would be saying Kaddish for my dad on his Yahrtzeit and again on Shabbat morning. Yahrtzeit from the Yiddish words yahr, which means year, and tzeit, which means time; literally translated it's anniversary.

Yitgadal v'Yitkadash, Sh'mey Rabah: Magnified and Sanctified be G-D's Great Name. How many times do I chant the full Kaddish or the half Kaddish over the course of the year as opposed to the three of four times a year that I intone the mourner's Kaddish? Hundreds, but here I stand, tears welling up in my eyes chanting the mourner's Kaddish seeing this vision of my dad's face, a big smile on his lips and a mischievous twinkle in his eyes.

During the first year after his death I acted in the play One Hundred Gates. I had Payes, wore a bekisheh, a gartel and a shtraymel, and as I was about to take my bow at the curtain call, I realized that I wouldn't be able to get a minyan to say Kaddish for Mincha. I waited a couple of minutes after the applause, walked out on stage and asked if I could get the minyan I needed. The audience, most of whom were filing out of the theater, turned and started to laugh. I told them that I would give everything I owned and all of my future possessions for that to be a joke.

One man shouted: "Can we daven on the stage?" So twenty or thirty men, with me leading the Mincha service while still in costume, davened on that stage. Friends of mine who stayed in the theater waiting to speak with me told me that it was the most surreal experience of their lives.

I have tons of stories about my dad and each one brings tears to my eyes, mostly tears of laughter.

We had a 1964 Rambler American: I used to call it the box, and if my dad didn't lend it to me, I took the subway. One night I had a date and asked him for the car; he wanted to know who my date was--he knew many of the girls I dated. I told him that he didn't know her, but he was insistent.

"What's her name?" he asked.
"You don't know her," I replied.

"I don't care," he said, "if you want the car, tell me her name?"

"Angie," I said not looking him in the eye.

He looked at me and said: "Angie, what's that short for?"

"Angela," I replied.

"Oh," he asked, "Angela what?"

"C'mon dad," I said," you don't know her, she lives in Manhattan."

Again he asked, "Angela what?"

I looked him straight in the eye and said: "Angela Famulare."

He replied, "Oh yeah, how are you getting there?"

He was a trip.

In 1965 I stopped asking him for the car. I was 20, well almost 20, when I got my first motor vehicle. It was a 150cc Suzuki motorcycle and I was tearing up the streets of Brooklyn challenging anybody with a bike to a race. Twelve races and nary a loss including one against a 1960 MGA all the way down Ocean Parkway into Coney Island.

"He was soloing Suzuki he was roaring down the street…Solo Suzuki…" I'd be singing their theme song as I rode; as a matter of fact, I still sing as I ride. My wife and I sing duets as we ride through the tunnels on our way into NYC. It's a little different now as my ride is a 1989 Harley Davidson bored out to ninety six cubic inches with roaring pipes, but the people driving next to us in the tunnels get a big kick out of it, and sometimes they even applaud; don't they know they're supposed to throw money?

Lenny Mandel

Back to 1966: this fellow on a Ducati 160 came up to me, accepted my challenge, and right there, right down Ocean Parkway we raced. I was lying flat on my ride; he was lying flat on his as well. We were booking this short quarter mile stretch with no lights, and I won! Ah, to triumph again, to raise my arms in victory once more, to laugh at the world, to marvel at my own immortality.

Just then this white Rambler American pulled up, and turned his wheel into my bike to cut me off. His bumper actually touched my front tire. Are the cops riding around in Ramblers now, I thought? No! He couldn't want to race me? Maybe he thinks that he's the Rambler in the song *Beep Beep* who catches up to the Cadillac to ask him how to get out of second gear? No such luck, the driver jumped out of his car, screamed at me about racing, put out his hand and demanded my keys.

I looked up at him and said, "C'mon dad, we're close to two miles from home, I can't push this bike two miles in this heat."

I handed him the keys, pulled the bike up onto the walkway and sat. My father got back in his car and drove away.

Pushing the bike two miles home in the heat didn't make me smile, nor was I going to leave it where it was, so I sat there until my dad was gone, added two or three minutes for safety, grabbed my wallet and pulled out my spare key. I hung out for a couple of hours at a friend's house, rode my bike to a friend's garage, walked through a sprinkler for effect, and went up to our apartment.
I walked in exhausted and covered with 'sweat', and there sat my father reading his newspaper at the kitchen table.

From Cross To Cross

He looked up at me and said, "Well son, I hope you've learned your lesson."

A few years before he died I asked him what his thoughts were on life after death.
"What happens to us when we die," I asked?
He looked me straight in the eyes and said: "When you die, you're dead."
I didn't understand what he was saying so I repeated the question and he repeated when you die, you're dead and then added: "They dress you in a shroud, put you in a plain pine box, bury you six feet below the ground and cover the casket with dirt, period."
"Wait a second," I said, "what about the after life, you know, heaven and hell?"
He looked at me incredulously and said: "Heaven and hell, are you kidding?"
I said: "I don't get it, if you don't believe in heaven and hell then why are you such an observant Jew?"
He smiled and said, "Hey, I could be wrong!"

It summed him up so beautifully that I sat there laughing my head off. He laughed as well.

Samuel Goldvasser lay dying in his bed, his young son, Reuven, standing by his side. As he began speaking his nostrils flared, he looked at Reuven and said, "My son, my dearest son, I can smell that mommy's baking rugelach. Please, I don't want to die without tasting her rugelach for the last time, run down and bring me a couple."

Reuven ran down the stairs and was back in a flash.
"Nu. Reuven," Samuel queried," where's the rugelach?"
Reuven looked at him and replied, "Mommy said they're for shiva!"

The day after my dad died, my mother and I sat in her kitchen; we talked, we laughed, and we cried; it was a wonderful catharsis. The doorbell rang, there was a delivery of desserts, among which was a box of rugelach. I started to laugh hysterically and then broke down in tears. My mother had no idea what was wrong.

I pointed to the rugelach and said, "That used to be one of the funniest jokes I knew."

My father died October 25, 1994. My mom spent every day and the entire weekend in the hospital sleeping on a reclining chair next to dad's bed. I came every day, a few hours each day, and we had a nurse there at night during the week; her name was Maddy and she was Jamaican. On the morning of October 25th my dad woke Maddy up screaming: my mom's name is Lotte, and Maddy, thinking he was calling her name, was jarred from her sleep.

She sat up and saw three men walk into the room and attempt to pull my dad from his bed. He was screaming "NO," but they continued. She described them to my mom: one was short with a long white beard, one nondescript and the third was tall with a moustache. When she jumped up to ask them what they wanted, they ran out of the room. The story was insane.

Dad's blood pressure dropped to sixty over thirty. He was bleeding internally and my mother was calling me frantically to get to the hospital. I was trying, but at 7:30 in the morning rush hour traffic into New York City was incredible. By the time I got there he was stabilized, I ran with the gurney to I.C.U. and the three of us spent his last few hours together.

A few days later, while we were sitting shiva, Maddy came over to pay respects. She walked into the den, saw a painting of my zeide on the wall and began to scream, "That's him, that's one of the men who was pulling Dave out of bed." She was hysterical and we were astounded. There was no way that she could have known what my zeide looked like; that he was a man with a long white beard, nor that my dad had two brothers, one very tall with a moustache and one nondescript, both of whom predeceased him. It gave us chills but in a way was very comforting. Maybe there really was an afterlife? G-D, I hoped so. I still hope so.

Let's go back to our ride. It's not that once you started to ride Deal's gap you'd have any time to think about anything but the ride; you didn't, so we stopped at the convenience store at its start. There had to be at least a little bit of time to shop.

> A man walks into a bar in Tel Aviv, and sees a very pretty lady sitting on the other side of the bar. He motions to the bartender.
> "Hey," he says, "do you have any Spanish Fly?"
> "Nope," the bartender replies, "we're in Israel. All we have is Jewish Fly!"

Lenny Mandel

The patron buys her a drink and pays the bartender who adds some of the 'Jewish Fly' to it.
Within five minutes the woman staggers over to him, puts her arm around his shoulder, puts her mouth next to his ear and whispers: "C'mon honey, let's go shopping."

Chapter 22
Deals Gap '94 and Now

Tee shirts, stickers for your bike, videos of Deal's Gap, pictures of myriad crashes-- motorcycles, cars, and trucks--post cards, all were for sale and the list was endless.

How could you go to one of the most famous stretches of road in the East without a souvenir? You can't and we didn't. We bought some tee shirts, a couple of 'dragon' stickers for the bikes, and we were ready to go. This wasn't my first encounter with Deal's Gap; I'd ridden it in 1994.

It was early in the morning of my first trip to Deal's Gap when four of us, all members of Northwest Jersey H.O.G., took off from Asheville, North Carolina. We stopped for breakfast at a small roadside eatery and began our jaunt.

Rolling hills and sweeping, majestic vistas led us through the back roads of Western North Carolina into Eastern Tennessee. Mike Ostenski, the director of our H.O.G. chapter, led the ride with Charlie, Wulf Sonne and me, and it was close to 10 a.m. when we reached the 'Crossroads of Time'--a small service station/convenience store that carried souvenirs, maps, various junk foods and gas. They were a bit surprised to see our big cruising motorcycles, as all the others there were riding sport and sport touring bikes.

    We spent a little time perusing the merchandise there, mounted up and rode off toward the gap. The turns on this road range from calm to hairpin and as you set up for a turn, the next one is in your face. It's an awesome ride, one that requires total concentration if you intend to do it at speed, which we did.
    We'd just come out of a sharp left when I heard the cracking of wood. Wulfie got caught on the edge of the blacktop and his bike was thrown into the underbrush and rocks on the side of the road. A quick glance in my mirror proved my fears to be accurate, but since the next turn was immediately upon us I had no time to reflect, just react. As I straightened out and began to slow down to a stop, there came Wulfie. No problem, I shot him a quick thumbs up and set up for the next turn.
    Somewhere around the nine mile marker there's a rest stop overlooking the gap, the river, and the beautiful Smokies. We stopped, caught our breath, and marveled at the ride we'd just taken. They were right; it is unbelievable.

    We finished the remaining couple of miles as if they were straight-aways and came out on a small road somewhere around Maryville, Tennessee. We were hungry and figured we'd stop at the next diner. Wrong, there was no diner in the area, but we happened upon a local joint and, being adventuresome, we decided to give it a try.
    There were four items on the menu: chicken n' dumplings, pork roast, ham steak or a hamburger. Since I

don't eat pork, and I wasn't going to try chopped meat in the woods of eastern Tennessee, I opted for the chicken. It was a mistake. The dish was swimming in a cream-like substance and was inedible. Wulfie ordered the same dish and the strains of Dueling Banjos in his ears forced him to eat. Well, I figured a piece of corn bread and a coke would have to hold me over. The boys ate their fill and we took off eastbound back to Asheville.

I don't remember who had the map, but we rode forty five miles in the wrong direction before we turned around. Don't misunderstand me I love to ride, and it doesn't matter if it's long, hard, fast, highway or scenic; today was different.

Mike saw a way to save lots of miles by cutting through the Smokey Mountains National Forest. It's gorgeous in the park and even though the riding is slower than on a highway, it's calmer and tranquility pervades (our pipes notwithstanding). About three-quarters of the way through the forest there was a blockade. The sign read: 'Eastbound Road Closed To Traffic'. I thought I'd puke. We had to backtrack through the park to end up on the highway we got off to save all those miles.

I was hungry, I was tired, I was pissed, I wanted something to eat, and I wanted it twenty minutes ago. I was dealing with this situation like a spoiled brat, pain in the ass child.

We rode through Pigeon Forge, which is a dry town loaded with touristy motels and such and headed, up the road a piece, to Gatlinburg. I spotted a Burger n' Brew, whipped my scoot into the parking lot, put my kickstand down, turned the bike off and headed for the door. The joint was open, and I ordered a burger, fries and a pint, before the door closed; I ordered all of this to an empty restaurant.

    Finally a woman called us to come upstairs, made us burgers and served beer in frosty mugs; it was wonderful. It could've been skunk-piss and I wouldn't have cared. We spent about an hour and a half there laughing at the day's events, eating and sucking down a couple of pints of brew. We thanked the woman profusely, and, as I was about to go asked how much further Asheville was.
"Oh, about twenty more miles," she replied. It'd been a very long day that started out gloriously and slowly became hellish, and I knew that the twenty miles would whiz by. Amen.
    We gassed up before the highway, hopped on route 40, and rode through the tunnel in the mountain that separates Tennessee and North Carolina. I sang as I rode knowing that the end of this hellish day was just about over. Asheville was right at other end of that tunnel.

    The sun hadn't yet set behind us as we rode east and, about a mile past the tunnel there was a big sign: Asheville fifty nine miles.
    The tears started running down my face, and Wulfie, knowing that I'd had enough, rode up to me. He looked at me and started laughing so hard I thought he'd fall off his scoot. I flipped him the bird, tweaked my throttle and sped off. The last fifty nine miles took forty five minutes and I didn't care; I would've welcomed a ride in a police car. We'd ridden five hundred miles and I was done.

Back at the hotel I parked in the spot marked 'employee of the month'. Wulfie pulled up a few minutes later, looked at me and began laughing again. We chained the bikes together and I started to laugh as well. Hey, we were parked, we were about to relax for the evening and I didn't even look like the employee of the month.

That was 1994 and I was riding solo and at speed. Here, in 2003, we were riding two-up (I had Shelly on the back) and I rode a huge cruiser. The first bike was a cruiser as well, but its configuration was very different. Shelly and Nedda weren't interested in speed; they were interested in staying in one piece, the bikes as well, so we rode slowly. It didn't really matter how slowly we rode, they were still holding on for dear life from mile one through mile eleven.

Somewhere around the nine-mile marker there were a half dozen or so motorcycles; each rider was taking a break or turning around to do it again. Not so for us, we knew that Tropical Storm Bill (remember that himicane) was all around us and we wanted to be in Lexington, Kentucky the next day, so we took off.

Route 129 joins route 441 just outside of Maryville, Tennessee, where we stopped for a quick drink, and the sky opened up once again. Rain or no rain, it was time for us to move our buns north.

When it's raining and you are trying to reach a specific destination, the scenery around you becomes less relevant than getting where you want to be, and doing it as quickly as possible. We caught I-75 around

Knoxville, so that we could make good time getting to the border of Kentucky.

Having quoted Shakespeare a few times I'd be remiss if I didn't include this story.

> Byron and Shakespeare die, go to heaven, meet St. Peter and tell him that they're ready to enter the kingdom of heaven. St Peter stops them and says: "Wait, I only have room for one poet in heaven, which one of you is going to stay?"
> "We're not poets," they answered in unison, "we're poet laureates. We've been translated into every language known to man and probably some not."
> "Yeah," St. Peter responded, "down there you guys are poet laureates, up here you're just poets and I only have room for one. I'll tell you what I'll do. We'll have a contest. Each of you will write a poem and the one who writes the better poem gets in."
> They each grabbed paper but before they began St. Peter added," There's one proviso, the poem must contain the word Timbuktu."
> Byron started writing, was finished in less than five minutes, handed his poem to St. Peter and said: "my poem is called The Desert."
> St. Peter read aloud:
>
>> "As we marched across the desert sands
>> a camel caravan came into view.
>> It stretched as far as the eye could see,
>> its destination, Timbuktu."

Shakespeare was flabbergasted, picked up his pen and began writing furiously. When he was done he handed the paper to St. Peter and said, "My poem is called the hunters."
Again St. Peter read aloud:

> *"Tim and I a hunting went*
> *when we spied three maidens in a tent.*
> *As they were three and we but two*
> *I buk one and Timbuktu."*

It's one of Shelly's favorites and if we strike up a conversation with other people at dinner and someone tells a joke, she asks for Shakespeare.

We exited I-75 in Jellico, North Carolina about a half a mile from the Kentucky border, and pulled into a motel right off the highway. We noticed that there was muddy footwear in front of every room: sneakers, work boots, and shoes. We looked at each other puzzled, wondering what we were about to encounter.

Chapter 23
Jellico, Tennessee, Heading to Kentucky

As per our daily ritual, I threw my swimsuit on and headed for the pool. Bob was already there and as I stood on the edge and dove in, the people standing around the pool began to laugh. Bob had been assuring me, and very loudly, that the water was warm; he lied. After a few choice words and a couple of laps in the pool I warmed up.

The people around the pool came over to talk to us and I was surprised to see lots of T-shirts with Jerry Garcia's picture on them (Jerry, of The Grateful Dead). As they got closer I could read the bold black lettering surrounding the face which read: Jesus is my Homeboy.'

"Here we go again," I thought to myself. Every T-shirt had, at the very least, a Cross on it; most had sayings, or quotes from Psalms along with a Cross.

These people were from Winston Salem, North Carolina, sent to build a home for a needy family. It sounded similar to Jimmy Carter's organization: Habitat for Humanity.

The shoes were put out there with hopes that they would dry before the next work day. There was no question in my mind that they worked as a team, one leader making sure that everyone was 'pulling in the same direction.'

I chuckled thinking about Yeshiva University's Crew.

> *Yeshiva University wanted to get involved in crew (like so many Jews row boats, right?). They found a bunch of students who were interested and would get up before morning prayers to practice in the East River.*
> *After months of practice the Rabbis couldn't figure out why their times were many minutes slower than all the other school's teams, so they sent one of their Rabbis to Boston to watch the Harvard crew at work.*
> *The phone rang in the Chancellor's office in New York: "NU?" he asked.*
> *The Rabbi, without waiting, answered, "I figured out the problem and it's easy," he said. "You see, at Harvard they have eight guys rowing and only one guy shouting!"*

They were very interested in our trip and Bob regaled them with some wonderful stories of the places we'd been and the riding we do. They asked Bob what he did for a living and he told them he was a barrister. When they asked about me, Bob and I looked at each other and laughed. What was he going to say? "That's my friend the Jew boy?" I was hoping that he wouldn't.

Bob told him that nobody really understood exactly what I did, and we all chuckled. Walking back to our rooms to dress and go to dinner there was a kid with a T-shirt that read: 'my boss is the son of a Jewish carpenter.'

"Wow," I thought, "he works for Pinocchio?"
You may think that it's irreverent, but not to me, I thought it was funny as hell, and laughed out loud once again. I seem to do that a lot when things strike me funny. My friend Paul Whelihan used to say: "I'm so funny I crack my own damn self up!" Me too.

Let's be honest, everybody says 'Jesus Christ'--it just depends on the situation--and it can mean many different things: Oh my G-D, holy shit, what the fuck--the list is endless. For me, for Jews, this is not blasphemous. Jesus is just another name, another Jew that the Romans tortured to death by crucifixion, and there were tens of thousands of us.
They say that the Jews, given the choice of who to save and who to crucify, screamed to free Barabas and crucify Jesus: how convenient.
I mean let's be realistic, if the early Christians had accused the Romans of killing Christ, the Romans would have wiped them out. The Jews didn't have that kind of power. That's why it was so easy for the Christians to make the Jews scapegoats.
Most Christians take the fact that everyone around them believes in Christ for granted. C'mon now, how many times do you walk into a store in December and the people working there say: "Merry Christmas?" For most of us it's most of the time.
My manager sent an e-mail to the office that we were having a Christmas/Holiday party. I wrote back: "We are either having a Holiday party, a Christmas party or a Christmas/Chanukah party. There are no other holidays that we celebrate at this time so make up your mind." The next e-mail we got was that the building management

would not allow us to have a 'Holiday-tree' trimming party. I, of course, wrote back: "There is no such thing as a Holiday tree, it is a Christmas tree. Would you please stop trying to be so p.c."

Back in the late 70's, I was driving through the town of Harrison, New Jersey, taking side streets to avoid the traffic on the main drag, when I saw a man lying on the ground. I stopped my car to see if I could help.
He was 'drunk as a skunk' (an expression that I never understood and still don't). I lifted him up and carried him to the corner where there was a small bar and grill.
My hands were full so I kicked the door, which they opened and helped me put him down on a table in one of the booths. They knew him and thanked me profusely for bringing him in: "You are a good Christian," one of them said to me.
I smiled and replied, "In Biblical terms, yes, thanks," and I left. Yeah, a good Christian, I thought as I walked back to my car. I wondered what they would have said if they knew I was a Jew. Oh, Oh I might have gotten another copy of the Journal American.

In Herb Gardner's play Conversations With My Father, the son is being 'called out' by a neighborhood punk and the father reads a note he found: "I got this note here; says—Dear Sheenie Bastard. Back of Carmine's, Remind you, Jewshit Joe, Eight o'clock A.M., Be There. Going to make Hamburger out of Goldberger…"
after a few lines the kid says:

"...but this DeSapio, he really hates me, this kid; he hated me the minute he saw me. He says we killed Christ, us Jews."

And the father answers: "They was all Jews there, kid, everybody; Christ, his mother, his whole crowd—you tell him there was a buncha Romans there too, makes him directly related to the guys done the actual hit!"

Now there's the truth, poetic though it may be, and I'd like to see them, today's Romans, finally own up to the deed once and for all.

> *Two Hasidic Jews worked in a retail religious articles shop. The neighborhood was changing: the Jewish families were moving out and Christian families moving in. They decided that in order to stay open they'd have to expand and start selling Christian religious articles. They had no clue as to what to buy so they opened the phone book, looked up under 'religious articles, Christian, wholesale' and dialed the number.*
> *"Can I help you," came the voice on the other side of the line.*
> *"Yes, hello, this is Isi Stein from Stein's religious articles in Brooklyn. My clientele is changing and I need to buy some crosses, but I have no idea about it."*
> *The voice on the other side of the line answered: "Mit or mit-out the Jesus?"*

Sister Rose Thering tells a story about a day in parochial school when she was about eleven years old. The nun teaching the class said: "Jesus said to his disciples, be wary of the Jews." Young Rose raised her hand and said: "how can that be possible Sister, they were all Jews."

Rose was sent home. Doesn't what she said make sense? It does to me.

Another one of my favorite stories happened on the way to a ski trip in Park City, Utah.

Thanksgiving of 1985, three of us decided to take our sons skiing in Northern Vermont; it was going to be a ski/bonding trip for us and our progeny. Well, Vermont didn't have any snow and while looking in the newspaper I found one hundred fifty nine dollar flights to Salt Lake City, Utah, so we changed our itinerary's alphabet one letter--from a V to a U--and headed west.

There was a lot of snow that November in Utah and I'd never skied out west, so...

There ended up to be eight of us that year as my friend Gary Shanker and his son Jonathan met us there, but the original six were: Roger Nakagawa with his son Ryan, Michael Chen with his son Alex, my son Wayne and, of course me. The limo picked us up at my house and we headed for Kennedy Airport.

There was tons of traffic and at one point the driver, attempting to make casual conversation, turned to the kids and said: "Well kids, what do you want for Christmas?"

Ryan Nakagawa, without skipping a beat said: "Are you kidding, you've got a Buddhist, a Shinto and a Jew in this car!"

We laughed for ten solid minutes, the limo driver laughed as well, and every time we'd look at Ryan we'd laugh again.

No matter where my thoughts were, my body was in Jellico, Tennessee and everyone was hungry, so we jumped on the bikes and rode to dinner. This would be the first dinner, on this trip, where we'd eat in a 'local joint,' as opposed to a national chain or an 'upscale joint' and I was looking forward to it.

We walked in: the twang of country music filled the air and the walls were covered with pictures: NASCAR drivers, Elvis, James Dean and more.

"We've got a special tonight," the waitress greeted us with that fabulous drawl. "All the ribs you can eat, $8.99, a dressed sweet potato and slaw."

I listen to southern women speak and I hear The Beach Boys line from California Girls "…and the southern girls with the way they talk, they knock me out when I'm down there." It's great and it's true.

Bob and Nedda went for the special and since I'm on a diet and don't eat pork anyway, I opted for a large salad, as did Shelly, and a large unsweetened ice tea.

People walked in wearing cowboy hats and boots and I'd have bet some were going to get up and do the Texas Two Step. I would've lost the bet but it would've been a pisser to be able to say that it happened.

People watching is a fabulous pastime and we really get a kick out of it; everybody there was getting a kick out of watching us as well.

At night Bob and I turn on special lights that we had installed on our bikes. Bob's are neon and make his bike look like a Wurlitzer juke box, and mine make my bike look like it's floating on a blue cloud; we don't think people look at us, we make sure of it.

It was fun pulling back into the motel. We watched the kids' eyes grow big and the smiles grow on their faces as they saw the glowing bikes in the dark night. It's wonderful to make people smile, and these bikes certainly do that.

> *It's the story of the two black guys walking down the street approaching a couple of Hasidim.*
> *One turns to the other and says: "What are they?"*
> *"Hasidim," his friend answers.*
> *He replies: "Ah see'd 'em too, but what are they?"*

On this trip, most of the places we stayed in included breakfast; some very nice, some continental and one, where's the nearest Waffle House? This motel had a nice assortment of breakfast foods and when Shelly and I walked in the next morning, Bob and Nedda were already in deep conversation with some locals about places to see and ride around Lexington, Kentucky.

Bob was adamant about staying off I-75 and finding nice back roads to get us to Lexington--after all we weren't in any hurry--but after talking to these people he conceded that the riding in the Lexington area would be where we should spend a lot of time so we boogied up I-75.

Chapter 24
Lexington Kentucky--Horse Country

Our first stop in Lexington was going to be the Horse Park, and from there we'd choose a route that would take us around the thoroughbred horse farms that, heretofore, we'd only heard about. There is no helmet law in Kentucky so mine was removed the minute I saw the 'Welcome to Kentucky' sign. We stopped before Lexington to gas up and, as Bob's bike automatically stops at Dairy Queen, we went there too.

I had no idea what the kid behind the counter was saying and made a comment about it. This initiated a long talk about the way I spoke as opposed to the way they spoke. I told them I was heading for Bourbon County; I love bourbon. The lady behind me said: "Sir, you're in the Bible belt, we don't drink here. Well, not in public anyway." It was a hoot.

Horses have always been one of my greatest loves; in my eyes the horse is the most beautiful animal in the world. I loved horses and dreamed of being a cowboy from the time I was four or five years old. I'd have been Shlepalong Goldberg, or some such name. I began riding when I was five and no jodhpurs, riding boots, jackets, cravats, silly hats or riding crop ever saw my body.

We were up in Canada and my pony's name was Bell (well, Bell really wasn't mine--she belonged to Mr. and Mrs. Matthews who owned Camp Bayview); I still have her saddle in the basement of my house. The summer that I learned that Bell died I was devastated, but it didn't temper my love of riding; I rode whenever I could.

During the eight weeks of camp I had to abide by the same rules as the other campers, but we usually stayed a couple of weeks after camp and you couldn't get me off the horses. I even rode in Brooklyn at Park Circle for two dollars an hour (an extra 50 cents got you a western saddle).

> *Morris went to the doctor and after a very thorough examination was told that he must do some kind of exercise.*
> *"What do you have in mind?" Morris queried.*
> *"Well," the doctor replied," why don't you go horse back riding in Central Park?"*
> *Morris' wife ran to Abercrombie and Fitch and bought him THE outfit: jodhpurs, riding boots, a white ruffled shirt, a red jacket and a riding cap. Morris came home from his first day in Central Park and said; "Sadie, they gave me, today, a stallion."*
> *"A stallion?" she asked, "how do you know?"*
> *"Because," Morris replied, ""everywhere I went, people pointed and said: "look at the shmuck on that horse!"*

I loved Hopalong Cassidy and was devastated when I found out that he was an actor and all the rest was bullshit; still I wanted to be a cowboy. Truth be told, what else was on TV when I was growing up? I watched every cowboy show on television.

 In 1983 I opened a horse farm in West Orange, New Jersey: Lazy L Farms; I was gonna live my dream!
 We had eleven acres and sixty three head of horses. I'd get up at six, hay the fields, hay and water the barns, make sure that the horses in the field got grain, did the same for the horses in the barn, went home, showered, got dressed and went to work at my day job.
 After work I went back to the barn, rode for an hour or two, made sure that all the horses were taken care of, chucked down a couple of beers with my boarders, hung around swapping stories and got home at around ten or eleven. I slept like a baby and couldn't wait to get up the next morning to start all over again.
 I wore a huge cowboy hat, chaps and my boots had spurs that jingle, jangle jingled. It was a trip and I loved taking it. To this day whenever I see a horse I see grace and beauty and I stop just to watch them move.

 The Lexington horse park is actually a museum although there are live horses on the property. John Henry and Cigar are there and you can go in and watch them get bathed--not something I needed to see--trust me I've bathed plenty of horses in my time. In any event I'd seen John Henry race and didn't need to see him, now in retirement, getting bathed. We bought some souvenirs at the horse park, took a picture at the statue of Secretariat and headed for the Blue Grass Driving Tour.

 Gorgeous, there is no other word to describe it: absolutely gorgeous. We rode these rolling hills, past lush farms and through beautiful countryside, and it seemed as if the horses in Kentucky live better than most of the state's human population. The scenic trail runs west, north and east of Lexington, skirting the city; if you are in that area it's a must.

Whenever I think of thoroughbred racing I remember when my dad took his mother, my bubby, to the racetrack at Saratoga Springs, New York. She told him to bet on the horse whose legs looked the best to her; go figure she was right and they won some money. You could always bet on bubby.

> A man came to see his grandson; he had a problem and wanted to talk. The grandson, a man already in his mid-forties took his zeide into the bedroom so that they could speak in private.
> "What's the matter, zeide?" he asked.
> His grandfather noticing a pill bottle on his grandson's dresser asked: "What are those pills?"
> "Zeide," he said," we're in here to talk about you, so talk."
> "I'm your grandfather," he said, "and I want to know what those pills are."
> "Viagra," the grandson replied.
> "What's Viagra for?" the zeide asked.
> Knowing that his zeide wouldn't stop until he had the answer the man said: "Viagra makes my sex life the same as it was when I was 25."
> Incredulous, the zeide asked: "Really, how much is each pill?"
> "Ten dollars," he replied.

They had their conversation and the zeide left. The next morning, when he awoke, he found one hundred and ten dollars under his pill bottle and immediately called his grandfather.
"Zeide, did you leave money under my pill box?"
"Yes," he replied, "I took one of your pills."
"But I told you, zeide, that the pills were only ten dollars."
"I know," the zeide replied," the hundred is from bubby."

What is a zeide? Pronounced ZIY-dee or zay-dee or zay-duh, depending on where your family is from, it means grandfather, but to BE a zeide was special.

My zeide was a beautiful man, with a long, stark white, flowing beard. He studied Torah, all Jewish law, and the prophets his entire life and lived as an ultra-orthodox Jew would, obeying all of G-D's commandments.

He lived Tevye's dream: he had the time to sit in the synagogue and pray, and the learned men discussed the holy books with him seven hours every day. Oh yes, he was rich, but not in the monetary sense. His life was filled with the richness of Torah and of Talmud making him the richest man of all.

In many American homes the zeide kept the family together, kept them involved with each other and with Judaism, and while he was alive nothing changed.

My zeide was a genius. Versed in every aspect of Jewish law, he was called upon all the time to clarify points that seemed muddled. When Hitler came to Vienna my zeide was forced to walk the streets of Vienna wearing a sandwich board sign on which was written: "Aryans: do not buy in Jewish shops." I pictured him, his beard stretched out in the breeze behind him, walking those streets.

    I used to walk with him in the Borough Park section of Brooklyn. He wore a long black coat and black hat, and I wore a pair of khaki chinos with a small Yarmulke bobby pinned to my head. The ultra orthodox boys would spit, as I walked by, livid at the fact that such a non-orthodox boy would be walking with such a righteous man. Zeide would smile, hold my arm a little tighter, and keep walking; he was much too smart to deal with petty nonsense.

    Normally if you're going to spit you spit directly at the person. These kids would spit on the ground to show their disdain. It wasn't so with the gentile kids who would spit right in your face.

    My zeide davened in a small, storefront synagogue, and when we, the kids, took a break, we'd play on the sidewalk right in front of the synagogue.

    I was about ten and my cousin Renee eleven, and we were playing some silly game when this strange girl and I bumped into each other. "Jew bastard," she mumbled; she grabbed me and tried to slap me. I backed up and she missed. My cousin Renee, taller than both of us (and beautiful) stepped in between us and squared off with her.

    The other girl snorted, threw her head back, 'hocked up a lugie,' and let it fly right at Renee. Renee ducked and I, standing right behind her, caught it square in the face.

From Cross To Cross

I cringe even now, more than forty five years later, thinking about it. I was a Jew Bastard! A Jew Bastard: what the hell is that?

Even though my zeide didn't live in my house, his presence was always felt. Moshe Yess wrote a song that speaks volumes:

> My zeide lived with us in my parents' home.
> He used to laugh, he put me on his knee.
> He spoke about his life in Poland,
> He spoke but with a bitter memory.
>
> He spoke about the soldiers who would beat him.
> They laughed at him they tore his long black coat.
> He spoke about a synagogue that they burnt down
> and the crying that was heard beneath the smoke.
> But zeide made us laugh, and zeide made us sing
> And zeide made a Kiddush Friday night.
> And zeide, O my zeide how I love him so.
> And zeide used to teach me wrong from right.
>
> His eyes lit up when he would teach me Torah.
> He taught me every line so carefully.
> He spoke about our slavery in Egypt.
> And how G-d took us out to make us free.
>
> But winter went by, summer came along
> I went to camp, to run and play
> And when I came back home they said "Zeide's gone"
> And all his books were packed and stored away.

Lenny Mandel

I don't know why and how it came to be,
It happened slowly over many years.
We just stopped being Jewish like my Zeide was
And no one cared enough to shed a tear.

Many winters went by, many summers came along
and now my children sit in front of me.
And who will be the Zeide of my children?
Who will be their Zeide if not me?

And who will be the zeide to our children? Those words bring tears rolling down my cheeks every time I hear them. We need zeides. Every Jewish family needs a zeide to keep us involved with, and enriched by, our heritage. What else is a zeide for?

I remember many years ago we took our son to Sammy's Rumanian--it's a restaurant on the lower east side of Manhattan that serves old world delicacies--and during the evening many Yiddish songs are sung. We sat there while at the next table an 'American bubby' was explaining the words to her two grandchildren. Her children had no idea what the songs meant and they were listening as well. I turned to Shelly and said: "when that bubby dies, any remnant of that family's Yiddishkeit is history." It was a very sad moment for me.

I thought of the Yiddish lullabies that my dad would sing to me at night, and hopefully I will be a zeide to my grandchildren and sing it to them as well. One of his favorites was Roshinkes Mit Mandlen (Raisins with Almonds).

From Cross To Cross

> In dem beis hamikdosh, in a vinkl cheider
> (In the Temple, in a corner of the room)
> Zitzt di almoneh, bas tzion alein
> (the widow Bas Tzion sits alone)
> Ihr ben yochidl yidel viegt zi keseder
> (her only son Yideleh, she rocks to sleep)
> Zingt ihm tzum shlofn a liedele shein
> (sings him, to sleep with a beautiful lullaby.)
> Unter yideles viegele, Shteit a klor vaise tzigele
> (Under little ones cradle in the night came a new little goat snowy white.)
> Dos tzigele iz gefohren handlen
> (The goat will go to the market)
> Dos vet zain dain beruf,
> (and Mother her watch will keep)
> Rozhinkes mit mandlen
> (raisins and almonds)
> Shlof-zshe yidele shlof
> (So sleep my little one, sleep.)

My father would always add ay-lu-lu-lu-lu.

These lyrics lose so much in translation and it's a shame that you can't hear the melody as you read. The song is actually a prophecy of becoming a tradesman; earning a very good living by buying and selling on the road and, if times get tough when you lie down to sleep, think of Raisins and Almonds; then sleep my little one, sleep.

The four of us wouldn't be getting to sleep until we reached West Virginia later that day. We were getting hungry so we stopped for lunch and went to gas up before our ride east towards the Daniel Boone National Forest.

CHAPTER 25
DID DANIEL BOONE EVER MEET A RACIST?

Not knowing the area, I took the map and walked into the convenience store. I asked if anyone knew any interesting back roads that we could ride, to and through, the forest.

We stood there talking about various routes when a man walked in. He was naked to the waist and I looked up to see that his chest was completely inked. In large gothic letters printed across his abdomen were the words: 'it's a white thing.' His arms were inked as well, but those words brought me to a reality that I didn't want to deal with. I looked up at him. I wanted to look him straight in the eye and at the same time I wanted to run away. I wish I could've read what the rest of the ink on his chest said but he'd already turned and walked out the door.

He never looked back and I never stopped looking.

On a ride with my friend Sonne nine years earlier, the ride in 1994 back from Asheville, we stopped for gas in Virginia and went into the convenience store there for a drink. Sonne was born in Germany and his father was in the Wehrmacht (something I didn't know until years later) during WWII. In the store was a young man with a swastika tattooed on his arm.

    Sonne saw me looking at this kid, and, knowing I was going to say something, pulled me out and said: "Listen, this isn't New York. You don't know anybody down here and that kid knows everybody. If you say or do anything to him, he'll be on the phone and we'll never get out of Virginia alive." I was steaming but he was right and I shut up.

    Now, right here in Lexington, Kentucky, I hoped that this 'white supremacist' wasn't listening to the route the four Jews were going to take to Daniel Boone. How the hell would he even know that we were Jewish?

    I am a professional actor and I get many calls to audition for an Italian, a Greek, a Russian or a Spaniard. I wonder if I changed the name on my resume to Lenny Mandolini for an Italian role, Leonis Mandikis for a Greek role or Leonardo Manuel Martinez for a Spanish one if anyone would know the difference. Would they still think that I 'look Jewish' then?

> *The phone rings in a condo in Miami Beach.*
> *A woman's answers-"Hello?"*
> *"Hi mom, it's Steven."*
> *"Steven?"*
> *"Yeah mom, your son, Steven, your only son."*
> *"Did you get a job yet?"*
> *"I'm an actor," he responds, "an actor."*
> *"Let me tell you something Stevie, an actor is not a job for a Jewish boy. A doctor, a lawyer, a teacher,*

> an accountant these are jobs for Jewish boys. Are you working on anything?"
> "Well, no, not at the moment."
> "Well call me when you get a job!" she says and she hangs up the phone.
> About six months later the phone rings again in the condo.
> "Hi mom," he says, "I'm just calling to let you know that I got a job. I'm starring in a new Broadway show."
> "Really," she asks, "what are you playing?"
> "I'm playing a Jewish husband," he replied."
> "Ha," she laughed, "you couldn't get a speaking role?"

    I'd played football on an amateur team which competed in a semi-pro league in 1966 when I lived in Florida and when I got back up north I continued.
    We were in the Greenpoint section of Brooklyn and the team we were playing was all Irish and Italian kids. Why are they Irish or Italian and I Jewish? Once again negating citizenship or country of heritage and dealing with my religion, and again I have the same problem with it; if I am a Jew, why is Tommy O'Leary not a Catholic or a Protestant, why is he Irish?

    One of the funniest things I ever heard was when Yogi Berra heard that the mayor of Dublin (right, that's Dublin, Ireland) was a Jew he said: "Only in America!"

    How many Jews play football to begin with? G-D Forbid you get hurt; what Jewish mother wanted her progeny playing that game anyway? My mom didn't, but I did, so I did. I was playing right guard on offense (and the long snap center) and middle guard (now called nose tackle) on defense.

The other team ran a sweep to the right and I pulled out to the left to follow the play. I got clipped by their tight end and as I lay on the ground holding my knee he bent over me and said, "That should hold you, Jew boy."

I mean, how did this guy know I was Jewish? Jew boy? Could he see that through my face guard? What was I missing? It goes back to the question that started this story: "Do I look Jewish?"

I asked the coach if I could switch to defensive end for a few plays and he agreed. I took the position facing the tight end and heard him again, "What's the matter Jew bastard (there I was again, a Jew bastard), didn't you get enough the last time?" He speared me right in the gut.

"C'mon ref," I said, "listen to the verbal abuse and watch the spearing" (which was illegal as well). After a series of downs, I'd had enough. The center snapped the ball but I paid no attention to the play: two spears to my gut and a string of Jew this and Jew that was enough. My entire being was focused on the tight end.

He came at me, I feinted (in no way to be confused with fainted) left, moved right and caught him, right under his chin strap, about an inch below my wrist. I snapped my arm straight out and felt his head move from my wrist all the way down my forearm to an inch or two above my elbow: the purest clothesline I'd ever done.

You could hear his neck snap across the field which, immediately, was festooned with laundry (the yellow flags that the referees used to signal fouls). Fifteen yards for the clothesline and fifteen more for..., well, whatever they called, I didn't care. I was ejected and he still hadn't moved. He lay on the field motionless and although I wanted to be upset I wasn't.

I felt like Morales, the girl from Puerto Rico in A Chorus Line, whose drama teacher, Mr. Karp, continuously taunted her and told her that she'd never be an actress because she couldn't feel anything. She relates her class history with him and finally she sings:

> "...six months later I heard that Karp had died
> and I dug right down to the bottom of my soul
> and cried... 'Cause I felt nothing."

As much as I felt that I should be upset, I wasn't; I gloated.

His teammates shouted at me and taunted me not to get back on the field, but I did a little dance step onto and off of the field from the sideline just to piss them off. It made no difference to me that I'd struck a blow for my own personal freedom. It made no difference to me that I'd struck a blow against the bull shit, a blow to let them see that some of us would not stand still and put up with their bigotry. Not even one little bit of difference.

When the game ended I asked my coach to let me know how the kid made out; I wanted to hurt him, I didn't want to cripple him.

It was different in Kentucky, very different. I assured myself that this guy knew that I was Jewish. Hell,

I assured myself that he knew that all of us were Jewish. It was a certainty that he was going to a meeting of his cronies and they were going to be waiting for us around Winchester or Mount Sterling: both towns along our route east.

I laughed thinking of the expression: "just because you're paranoid doesn't mean that we're not really following you!" The laugh didn't last very long. White power, sieg heil, skinheads, Nazis and neo-Nazis: all these images ran through my mind. It was quite a difference being out of my safety net, out of the northeast; the fear was palpable.

I tell people that when I ride most people leave me alone because they can't tell if I'm a Rabbi or a member of the Hell's Angels; it keeps me out of trouble. Here it wouldn't have made one bit of difference.

Today's bikers, I'm talking about the Harley guys, the 'tough guys,' are a new breed. Most are about as tough as a cream puff, but they make sure that they look the part.

There are many of us, bikers to the core, who love to ride and do, whenever possible, putting thousands of miles on our bikes each year. There are, as well, plenty of outlaw gangs that not only look the part but play the part as well. For you the difference is not very obvious, for me it's a piece of cake.

Whenever I want a good chuckle, I mosey on down to any local 'biker bar' and watch the people attempt to perpetuate the hard-core biker myth.

They'll be showing off their latest ink, wearing jeans with just the right amount of tears, a do-rag, and a black

T-shirt with some inane saying on it, and they look tough. Yeah, they can spit nails; that's right, chew 'em down to the head and spit 'em out. Don't forget black boots and heavy chains from belt loops to wallets; most of which contain gold American Express cards and a local PBA card, and their helmets sport the latest in tough guy stickers.

They ride down the street snapping their throttles, to hear their exhaust pipes cracking like so many whips; this is even more fun in tunnels or on crowded streets, where you can probably get a dozen or more car alarms to go off, and it's done with a huge scowl: 'the face,' I call it.

Monday, Monday, so what happens Monday? On Monday most of these guys put on suits, shirts and ties and go to work. They are accountants, stockbrokers, bank tellers, freight forwarders, the list is endless. Friends of mine watch as these 'tough guys' walk toward me at these bars. Many of them look at me, nod acknowledgment and quickly avert their eyes. It's truly comical.

I was walking around Sedona, Arizona a few years ago, noticed a quaint jewelry store and went in. I was dressed in my usual 'mythical' outfit: my hair was long--on that day I let my pony-tail out--and I was wearing a T-shirt with the logo: 'Ice Cream Man From Hell' written on it. It Is a picture of a skull, engulfed in flames, eating an ice cream pop, surrounded by the name.

The two women standing behind the counter wouldn't take their eyes off of me as I walked around the store.

In one of the display cases I saw a necklace that I liked and asked to see it (I think they flipped a coin and the loser had to wait on me while the other one kept her foot on the alarm button).

The 'loser of the flip' came over to me and in a trembling, soft as silk voice asked what I wanted to see. I pointed to the necklace; it was a beautiful, multi-colored, beaded piece. She explained that the piece was one-of-a-kind, done by a local craftsman and had been hand made from Peyote buds.

I began to chuckle and then to laugh; my laugh is warm and infectious.

At that exact moment the woman hauled off and punched me.

"Why you're nothing but a big Teddy Bear," she screamed. "You come in here looking like a Grizzly Bear, and you're a fucking Teddy Bear." She cocked her arm again and I exclaimed: "don't hit me again, it'd be a mistake."

The three of us laughed till tears ran down our faces.

That was me, but here was a guy, this white power guy, who wasn't perpetuating any myth. This guy was the real deal and, for the first time on this trip, I felt insecure; it sucked. I wasn't looking for my mommy, my stuffed teddy or my blanky, but any one of the three might've helped.

"Toto," I thought, "I have a feeling that we're not in Kansas anymore." I chuckled realizing that being in Kansas, with regard to white supremacists, probably wouldn't be much different than being in Kentucky.

When I've had enough of a situation and it's time to move on, I always tell the same story.

> *A man goes to the doctor.*
> *"Doc," he says, "I can't pee."*
> *"How old are you?" the doctor asks.*
> *"96," the man replies.*
> *The doctor looks at him and says: "You peed enough!"*

I wanted to stop thinking of this guy. I desperately wanted to rid my mind of the ink on his belly. I peed enough, really, really, really- I PEED ENOUGH!!!

I was cursing Rabbi Kiel's comment about not being able to control your thoughts and wished, no prayed that I could control them now. I wondered if these were past-life events that still haunted me. Past life events-- reincarnation? Most people, hell, most Jews don't know that the concept exists for us.

The Midrash tells us that we were all together at Mt. Sinai when G-D gave us the Torah: if that is true than we must believe in re-incarnation. How else could it be possible for all of us to have been there and be alive today? I have always believed in re-incarnation anyway.

There are six hundred thirteen Mitzvot that every Jew must do. Some are only for men, some for women, some for the Cohanim, some for the Levites, some for the King and the one that transcends them all is to die for your beliefs (martyrdom). So one must assume that you have to keep coming back until you have achieved all six hundred thirteen and then you attain paradise: sounds like reincarnation, no?

Maybe all of my feelings and fears about Judaism and being Jewish stem from all the persecution over time, that, according to the re-incarnation theory, I have lived through. Well, it's a thought.

When you die your soul goes back to G-D. There are billions of souls, so where does he keep them? The place is called the Guf.

When a baby is born G-D has a soul brought from the Guf and that soul goes into the mother's womb. Before one leaves the womb an angel places his finger over the center of your mouth, all of your previous memory is wiped away and all that's left is the mark of the angel's finger above your lips.

How about the baby boom, 1946 to 1965? There were seventy six million American babies born during the post-World War II baby boom, an increase of more than seventeen million babies over previous time periods.

You must think that all the G.I.'s coming home from the war wanted to start families, and you're probably right, but where did all these excess souls come from? How about the eleven plus million people killed during WWII? C'mon, think about it. Isn't it a possibility?
Yeah, past-life events or maybe it was just the stories I grew up with running through my mind. In any case I felt miserable.

From Lexington we rode route 60 east, it parallels I-64 and it's a much prettier route. When we got to Winchester, Kentucky, I kept turning my head around looking for 'Mr. white-power's' van; I knew I'd never see it again, I mean I really knew it, but that didn't stop me from looking for it. I thought about his ink.

From Cross To Cross

These were no jailhouse tattoos, these were professionally done. Wearing them and, more specifically, displaying them the way he did was putting it in your face; he had nothing to hide and he feared nothing. It was like throwing down the gauntlet and seeing who had the balls to pick it up and accept the challenge. Years ago on my home turf, it would have been me. Hell, right now if that had been on my home turf it would have been me.

CHAPTER 26
Day Six Mid-Day heading for West Virginia

The towns and the villages that you pass through are what make riding the back roads of rural America so great. Each has its own distinct flavor and what would a trip like this be if you couldn't taste each individual morsel?

Our decision was to ride to and through a portion of the Daniel Boone National Forest, get on I-64 and spend the night around Huntington, West Virginia. "West Virginia," I thought, "now there's a state full of good ol' boys, maybe we should just drive through the night into Pennsylvania?" I laughed at myself again but not very loudly this time; it wasn't even a remote possibility.

We turned off route 60 onto 460, which is half the size of 60, heading for Frenchburg, Kentucky and the Daniel Boone National Forest. The farther we rode the louder that banjo picking got. Bob wanted an interesting ride before we hit the interstate so I obliged him.

We turned onto route 36 in Frenchburg and made an immediate turn onto route 1274; it was, as luck would have it, the right move. What a gorgeous road. Route 1274 ran past hewn cliffs on one side, trees and fields on the other. It had rolling hills and wonderful curves that swept us along finally coming to, and riding along a lake.

Lakes don't have straight lines and either did this road which turned into old route 1274, and we rode up the mountain on this blacktop highway.
It was slower going and I thought, this surely is the 'backwoods' of Kentucky.

Old 1274 ended and we turned onto route 519 north, where the first sign we saw was for Morehead State University; we smiled. We are fans of the football Giants and Phil Simms, their old quarterback, went to school there.

Once on I-64 I twisted the throttle while Bob hung back. I knew that if we stayed in the flow of traffic we'd never get a ticket, but he told me about the wolf-packs that stalked the highways. I laughed, but he explained that wolf-packs were anywhere from five to ten police cars that pulled over all of the cars that were speeding--the entire flow of traffic--at once.

I was chuckling about it until I saw the strobes of police cars on the side of the road. I slowed to about seventy miles an hour. There were more strobes, more, and even more: all in all there were seven police cars within forty or fifty yards. I realized that the wolf-pack story has more validity than the Werewolf story. Well, at least I've already seen the wolf-pack.

About a mile before West Virginia traffic stopped, and it was stopped as far as I could see. I turned onto the left shoulder and hung a U-Turn over the median, heading back west from where we'd just come. Bob was right on my heels and we got off immediately riding route 23 north.

From Cross To Cross

We were going to spend the night in Kentucky after all, Ashland, Kentucky. It was July 3rd.

Chapter 27
Erev Independence Day

I love to tease people so when Bobby tells them that he's Canadian I always ask them if Canada has July the 4th. Believe it or not, most people say no, so I ask if the Canadian calendar actually goes from July the 3rd to July the 5th with nothing in between. It's funny; try it.

Another one that I love to use is: "there is a street in New York City spelled H-O-U-S-T-O-N, pronounced HOWSTEN. What's the capital of Texas?" Most people (and many look at you with an expression of 'how dare you think me to be stupid') immediately say Houston; the answer of course is Austin.

It had been a long day, physically as well as mentally, and we were all looking forward to a good night sleep. I kept looking for that white van and hoped I could get to sleep knowing that 'he' was driving around looking for me. We pulled into a Holiday Inn Express located next to two railroad crossings.

What we didn't know was that trains have to blow their whistles when they approach these crossings and we had to sign a release acknowledging that before we checked in. To the girls' chagrin Bob and I decided to take a quick dip before going to dinner.

This was a bone of contention for both Shelly and Nedda the whole trip, although they didn't make it known until Jellico.
I'm not talking about the pool; I'm talking about the riding until eight so we never ate before nine. Shelly was adamant, so the rule for all rides from now on is that we can ride as long as we want as long as we stop for dinner by seven.

Shelly is very beautiful, dresses very well and accessorizes to the Nth—she's a fashion plate. On our motorcycle trips, however, she's only allowed one extra pair of jeans and underwear for the length of the trip; she can bring as many tops as she likes. I ask that her jewelry be very, very simple and if she wore nothing but a plain wedding band and small earrings it would be more than enough. After all these years she deals with the clothing (or lack thereof) very well; the jewelry issue is a killer for her.
It's not that her jewelry is gaudy or flashy, it's not, it's very beautiful, very tasteful and, for the most part, she plays it down. There's just no reason to wear expensive jewelry on the road, when you're trying to play yourselves down: bikers not R.U.B.s (rich urban bikers--the connotation is the same as the helmet sticker that reads: '1500 miles and fifteen thousand dollars don't make you a biker'). People look at her and would never even consider that this freckle faced redhead with gray-green eyes could be anything but a colleen of Irish descent: they're wrong!

A spaceship lands in the middle of New York City's Central Park. Every news agency is there as the hatch opens and a red creature, with no eyes, two

antennae sticking up out of its 'head' and covered with jewels emerges.
Mike Wallace walks forward, asks if it understands our language, and if so could he ask a few questions.
The creature nods and Mike begins:
"Where are you from?" he asks.
"I'm from Mars," comes the response.
"Mars?" he asks, "we thought all Martians were green!"
"Well," the Martian replies, "we used to be green but the Sun got too close and scorched us and now we are all red."
"But you have no eyes," Mike comments.
"Not a problem," the Martian replies, "we experience all the senses with our antennae. I promise you we don't miss a thing."
"And," Mike continues, "are all Martians so covered with diamonds and emeralds and sapphires and rubies?"
The Martian lifts his head as if to look him straight in the eyes and says: "not the gentiles."

There was a week long July 4th celebration in Ashland and the pier was jammed with people as we rode by heading for dinner. The Doobie Brothers were playing that night and searchlights from helicopters scoured the river, looking for kids drinking in their boats. We pulled into the parking lot of Texas Roadhouse; it was wall-to-wall cars and bikes. The Texas Roadhouse is a restaurant chain that hasn't made it as far East as New Jersey yet; it should.

When we were seated, the incongruities of the ambience within made all of us laugh. Here we were chucking peanut shells on the ground, listening to the twang of country music while the TV showed Serena Williams kicking someone's butt at Wimbledon.

Everyone said the food was great; I had a salad with squeezed lemon for my dressing.

When we mounted up after dinner, we flipped on our 'neons,' and rode back to the motel. Don't think that I'd forgotten about my 'white supremacist' and his van—no shot.

I was ecstatic that there were a bunch of motorcycles in the parking lot and all in front of rooms on the first floor, DUH, (what would they do, ride them up the stairs to the next level?). We were on the second floor.

"To sleep, perchance to dream..." there I go quoting Willie again. I was looking forward to a good night's sleep, the 'guy' notwithstanding. C'mon, be realistic, he wasn't following us, he wasn't calling his minions to look for us, he didn't know, nor did he care that we even existed. It took a while but I dozed off.

TOOOOOOOOOOOOOOOOO, TOOOOOOOO TOOOOOOOOOOO, I heard the first two whistles at around midnight. I closed my eyes and tried to get back to sleep.

TOOOOOOOOOOOOOOOOO, TOOOOOOOO TOOOOOOOOOOO, I was wide-awake; it was one a.m. Whoa, I thought, this is going to be a night.

The trains ran all night. I fell asleep around four in the morning and slept until about eight thirty; it wasn't

From Cross To Cross

enough and I knew that this was going to be my day, Lenny the grinch day, and it wasn't going to be pretty.

The next day, Friday July 4th, Independence Day, we headed north-northeast towards Pennsylvania.

Chapter 28
July 4th Pennsylvania Here We come

The Ohio River is the natural boundary of West Virginia, Kentucky, Ohio and Pennsylvania and the difference on which side of the river you rode on depended upon your feelings about wearing a helmet. No one else cared so I opted for the Kentucky and Ohio side; they don't have helmet laws and I wanted to ride 'topless.'

In 1993 Shelly and I rode up to Lincoln, New Hampshire for the Northeast H.O.G. rally. It was already dark when we crossed into New Hampshire. We had to stop for gas, and I strapped my helmet to the back of the bike; Shelly wouldn't dare. It was a gorgeous night. The sky was pitch-black with a gazillion stars; it felt like camp. No soot, no pollution, and no lights from tall buildings taking away from the beauty that G-D bestowed on us; it was fantastic.

We hooked up with hundreds of bikes heading north, got to Loon, N.H., checked into our hotel and, being that we hadn't eaten in several hours, went downstairs to grab a quick bite. The restaurant was closed and the closest open eateries were in town about a mile or two away so we rode into town helmet-less; she loved it and rode most of the trip without it. Now, unless it's a real short ride she wears it. I don't know what difference a small ride makes.

It's the story of the idiot (and, no, I am not calling Shelly an idiot) who, when he read that most accidents occur within fifteen minutes of home, moved!
Either you're gonna' wear a helmet or you're not!

We rode out of Ashland, headed south then east, rode into West Virginia for thirty seconds or so, shot over a bridge and we were in Ohio heading North on route 7. Being in Ohio calmed me and my Jewish-ness. Maybe it had to do with the large Jewish population at Ohio State University, maybe it had to do with Ohio being a part of the Union during the Civil War. Go figure--I haven't been able to.

Ohio route 7 ran north along the west bank of the Ohio River; route 2 paralleled it on the West Virginia side. Barges laden with coal heading north and barges laden with coal heading south along with pleasure boats, powerboats and lots of people out on wave runners, crowded the river. There was a suspension bridge the likes of which none of us had ever seen and we stopped to marvel at the engineering. We rode through quaint towns with more churches, and nary a synagogue to be found.

That was Hitler's plan as well, nary a Jew to be found and their synagogues rubble. No traces of Judaism ever. If the Nazis found you with any trace of Jewish blood you were sent to the camps.

One Sunday morning Mass the Nazis marched into the church and declared: "All Jews step outside. Anyone whose grandfather was a Jew go out. Anyone whose grandmother was a Jew, go out. Anyone whose father was a Jew, step out. Lastly, any of you whose mother was a Jew step outside."
With that the Priest grabbed the crucifix, off the wall and while cradling it in his arms said: "All right brother, it's time for us to go too."

We crossed the Ohio River at Gallipolis, rode route 2 on the West Virginia side, and decided to stop at a truck stop at Point Pleasant, West Virginia, for a bite to eat.

Truck stops are interesting places as the store there carries all kinds of goodies for one's rig: flashing lights, strobes, multi colored lights, c b radios, cushions, stickers, the list is endless. There was a bumper sticker with a picture of a girl inside a circle with a line through it: "No Lot Lizards," it read. Lot lizards, now there's a term I'd never heard before, but looking at the way the girl in the circle was dressed I figured she was a hooker; I was right.

When Wayne was about five years old we drove into New York City to watch a New York Ranger hockey game. We were stopped at a light when a woman motioned to me from the curb. In the old days I would've kibitzed with her as a goof but with my son in the car: no shot. I pointed to my son sitting in the passenger seat but she thought I was motioning her to get in. She walked over to the car and as she was about to open the door she saw Wayne, gasped and jumped back.

Wayne looked at me and asked: "Who is that, daddy?"

"She's a hooker," I replied.

"You mean she works in a rug factory?" he asked?

I laughed for ten minutes. Actually, I laughed the entire night.

A man goes to a brothel, and takes off his coat. As if by magic, twelve luscious beauties line the stairs.

"Which one strikes your fancy?" the madam asks. The man looks and says: "Which one is Becky Cohen?"

Incredulous, the madam replies: "Becky Cohen? You've got to be joking. No one asks for Becky. She has no talent, if you know what I mean?"

He was adamant and the madam took him to Becky's room.

When they were finished the man gave Becky one hundred dollars.

Becky, not used to getting anything, was overjoyed. The next day he returned, and again the twelve luscious beauties appeared on the stairs.

"Which one strikes your fancy today?" she asked.

"I want Becky Cohen again," he replied.

The madam didn't question and took him to Becky's room again, and again, when they were finished, the man gave Becky one hundred dollars.

This went on for three weeks and one night he turned to Becky and said: "I won't be seeing you anymore, Becky."

"Why not?" she asked.

"I'm going home," he replied.
"Home?" she asked, "where do you live?"
"I live in Israel," he answered.
"Wow," she said, "my mother lives in Israel."
"I know," he said, "she gave me twenty one hundred dollars to give you."

According to Bobby this particular truck stop was a dump. I didn't care; I was having a diet coke and a half of a glass of hot water anyway. A half of a glass of hot water: a gleyzele tea, now there's an ethnic concept.

I'd love to hear one of the 'horsey-set' finish dinner and ask for a glass of tea instead of a cup of tea. I can just hear the maitre d' at The Plaza in New York City: "may I offer you a glass of chamomile?"

I'd spent long enough at this truck stop, duh, so we mounted up and decided to ride along the river a little longer, jump onto route 50 east, and then north on I-79 to make some time. I was in the lead, dancing and singing as we rode and I missed the cut off for route 50. It's not like it was a tiny sign hidden by a bush. It was a huge road sign and Bobby was beeping his horn and flashing his lights, to no avail. He pulled up next to me letting me know I'd passed route 50 but there was no place to turn back. We rode to the next exit.

Bob had the map and decided that we'd ride route 2 a couple of miles longer then jump on route 16 which would bring us back to route 50. I'd already decided that we'd turn around and go back the way we came, but Bob was adamant. We were thirty yards away from each other and he turned his bike and headed north.

Lenny Mandel

'Lenny-the-bitch-day' was about to begin--you know exactly what I mean; you're tired, you haven't eaten and you're not getting your way--watch out. This rarely happens to me on the bike. The bike is my shrink, my therapist, the place where I can be alone in my own head surrounded by nature. The last time was also on a ride down south. It was in 1994, the day we rode Deal's Gap the first time.

On the map, route 16 appeared to be a couple of miles up route 2 and Bobby, now leading our little pack, sped along. No doubt he sensed my intense bitchiness and knew the explosion was near. Well, two or three miles turned into seventeen or eighteen miles and I was seething, I mean SEETHING! Scenery? What's that?

Chapter 29
Mid-day day seven-
Lenny is a Bitch day

Riding up route 2 there was a sight I'd never seen before other than in pictures-- a nuclear power plant. It distracted me from my 'pissed-offednes.'
We slowed down and Shelly and I talked about it. It reminded me of the scene in Tootsie where Dustin Hoffman is in Sidney Pollack's office telling him that he was going to raise the money to put his roommate's play on. I'm paraphrasing. Sidney screams at him and says: "…no one is going to sit and watch some play about toxic waste. If they want to see toxic waste they could go out to New Jersey…" I laughed when I saw it and laugh now thinking about it. Shelly, on the other hand, born and raised in New Jersey, doesn't find it amusing at all.

When people ask me where I'm from I always say New York City. This pisses Shelly off immeasurably, as we live in New Jersey, but I'm from the city and, geographically, it gives them a better shot of knowing where we live (if you believe that, I've got a bridge for sale in Brooklyn).

Finally we got to route 16; Bob slowed down and motioned for me to lead. Without acknowledging him I grabbed the throttle and roared past. Route 16 ended up to be an exceptional road, twisting, turning and following a slightly mountainous track. I was flying and although I glanced in the mirror to see if Bob and Nedda were in sight, I knew that even though I couldn't see them, they were far behind us. That's the way I wanted it anyway so I could blow off steam on this stretch of road; I did.

There was a gas station at the junction of route 50. I needed gas and I wasn't going to jump on route 50 without them, so I waited. Bob pulled onto 50 without a blink. "Here we go again," I thought. Screw it, I followed him onto the highway and passed him doing about eighty miles an hour.

When you ride in a pack the leader always points out objects in the road that might be dangerous to the riders behind him. This is done by pointing a toe, or circling your foot around the spot, and it continues from rider to rider until the last rider is notified. There was a dead animal on the road and I stuck my foot out and pointed to it to let Bob know it was there.

I got off at the next exit as it showed that there was a gas station there, pulled up to the pump and began filling up. Bob pulled in behind me but chose a pump on the other side and one back; not a word was spoken.

The girls were in the convenience store as Bob walked up to me and said: "I apologize, I'm truly sorry, I made a choice, it was the wrong choice, and it was a mistake." Okay so when he reads this he's going to dispute part of it but he did apologize. We gave each other a big bear hug (and, like I mentioned before, we are two bears) and a kiss. He said that he knew how pissed I was and that he knew that he was forgiven when I pointed out the dead animal in the road. We decided to ride route 50 quickly to get to I-79; our destination was State College, Pennsylvania.

Shelly and I wanted to be home by Saturday night to catch up on eight days of mail etc., and Bobby figured that State College was about equidistant from both Toronto and New York City, so it was agreed that that's where we'd spend the night before our ride back home.

The sky was getting darker as we rode north. As it wasn't evening and we'd seen these skies many times before, we turned onto I-68 instead of taking back roads. The interstate highways down here are very scenic, but they lack the twists and turns and the flavor of the small towns we ride through while on back roads. We were trying to make time and knew there'd be smaller roads once we left the interstate.

The sky went from darker to Oh, Oh, and we pulled under an overpass just as the rain started falling. We'd been through this drill so many times on this ride that we just laughed, pulled out the rain gear once again, and rode on; of course the rain stopped ten minutes later.

I-68 ran us back into western Maryland and in Cumberland we headed north, jumping onto route 220: another great road to ride. Route 220 had rolling hills, turns galore and short dips in the road, which took us past pastures and small shops; it felt great. Since the deal now was to eat before seven we made tracks for Altoona, Pa. and stopped for dinner.

Lenny Mandel

A household name, this upscale chain was right off the highway with a motel right behind it. Bob looked at me and said: "It's just a suggestion, but I'd have no problem seeing if there are any vacancies here and calling it a day." We all agreed.

It was a wonderful meal and as we sat there laughing we knew that we were done. It was a very long day, we'd put on a lot of miles and I only had one real bitchy moment. We laughed about that as well.

The motel was beautiful; one of the most upscale I've ever seen. The girls relaxed and Bobby and I moseyed down to the pool.
Why was this night different from all other nights? On this night we didn't have to rush out of the pool, dry off, get on the bikes and go to dinner. We'd already eaten.
The pool was beautifully shaped and deep, with a hot tub one level above, embedded in rocks. Bob and I hung out in the pool, talked about the day, about the trip, about our lives and about this book. Nedda came down and dove in as well. I shared my ideas for the title of this piece and he said, "What about From Cross to Cross?" I loved it--hey, I used it, didn't I?

Chapter 30
The Morning of Day Eight

We had a wonderful night's sleep and when we woke up I was ready to go. We walked across the street to Friendly's--I had my usual and so did they. We packed our bikes, gave each other big hugs and kisses, bade each other safe home, and the usual 'keep the rubber side down,' mounted up and rode off onto I-99.

We rode the first few miles together as we'd been doing the whole trip and then Bob and Nedda veered off onto route 865 heading north towards home.

It takes a while to get used to riding alone after spending so much time on the road with other bikes, or just one other bike as was the case here. Shelly wasn't interested in whipping back roads today, she just wanted to get home; I didn't argue. There are times after a long ride that I point the bike homeward and get 'back to the barn syndrome'. It's the term we use when tired, overridden hack horses, plodding along the same boring trail hour after hour, perk up their ears and pick up a strong and noticeably quicker gait, when you turn them for home. They know that the sooner they get you there the sooner they are done (actually they think they are going to eat).

I-99 becomes route 220 again and finally we connected with I-80 (which we in The Garden State call route 80). I set the cruise control to seventy eight miles an hour, cranked up the volume on the stereo and sat back for the two hundred fifty plus mile ride home. With stops I figured we were looking at five, maybe five and a half, hours and my mind, as it always does, wandered.

How my life has changed! As someone once said: "who woulda thunk it?"
How it had evolved from growing up in an observant home to moving away from the observance but never from the culture. I always maintained a very strong Jewish identity, no matter my situation. I think that the solidifying factor for that was my trip to Israel in the summer of 1962; my heart never beat stronger and I never felt prouder than after that trip.

It was on that trip to Israel in 1962 that I really met my great aunt Bracha; she was my dad's aunt and she just passed away a couple of months ago. I wrote a eulogy for her.

My son lost his great-great-aunt Bracha today; she was my great-aunt and, obviously, my father's aunt: although she was only eighteen months older than he.
I haven't yet figured out why I have tears streaming down my cheek when I should have a huge grin on my face celebrating her life, the way she lived, her family, her friends, her choices, and her age.

From Cross To Cross

Born in Poland, Bracha Koren, nee Mandel, was the youngest of ten children, the sister of my grandfather Wolf, who was the oldest sibling.

While her two oldest siblings were ultra-orthodox, dodah Bracha went all the way to the left politically and religiously, and she became active in a Socialist group, HaShomer Hatzair. I'm sure that aside from it being an escape from the religious lifestyle of her parents, it was a great social outlet, a wonderful way to meet new people and, especially boys. It must've been an interesting change--frumkeit to Socialism--and the fights at that dinner table (and everywhere else in the house) must've been astounding.

In 1930, at the ripe old age of twenty two, Bracha emigrated to Palestine where she settled on Kibbutz Mizrah. It was in Emek Yisrael right down the mountain from Nazareth. It was here, on this Hashomer Hatzair Kibbutz, that she met Asher Koren and they were married.

It was very rough but they were the Chalutzim, they were the builders of the land, and they knew that they could make this 'desert' bloom. Did they ever; orchards and vines, milk cows and goats thrived in this, heretofore, dust bowl. There were problems with the British, the Turks, the Arabs, the French and the religious Jews, but Mizrah thrived.

HaShomer Hatzair didn't allow alcoholic beverages, nor did it allow dance-hall type dancing. It was pure, it was idealistic, they had a dream and they were living it.

Bracha and Asher had three children, Ziva, Gadi and Tzofi, and Bracha lived to see many grandchildren and great-grandchildren.

Life on the kibbutz was living with your family and watching them grow. It was never a matter of getting up and leaving 'kibbutz-life' to go to Tel-Aviv or Haifa to live.

No, you raised your children right there, and, up until recently it stayed that way. You danced at every joyous occasion and wept at sorrowful ones. Your neighbors were your family as well.

I remember the summer of 1962 as if it were yesterday. I was fifteen and a half and on a plane for Israel to spend the summer with my family, my Israeli family. I'd only met my aunt Bracha once; I was four and a half so my recollection of her was negligible at best.

We landed at Lod (now Ben Gurion) airport and aunt Bracha was there along with another cousin of mine, Joseph Amir, who was the under-secretary of the treasury in Israel.

> *A man landed at Ben-Gurion Airport and the customs agent asked him to open one of his bags. The agent, seeing that the bag was full of cash in various currencies, asked where all the money came from.*
> *"I went into men's bathrooms all over the world," he answered, "grabbed each man and told him that if he didn't contribute to the safety and well-being of Israel, I would cut his balls off!"*
> *"What's in the other bag," the customs agent asked?*

From Cross To Cross

> "Well," the man said," you'd be surprised how many men don't give a damn about Israel's well-being."

    Joseph was a dapper, well groomed man, with a cigarette dangling from his mouth. He pointed to my suitcase and a man in uniform walked it (and me) right through customs. It was as if I were a diplomat.
    Standing next to him was an 'old lady'. Ironically, she was the same age then that I am now. She had close-cropped gray hair, no make up, the look of a hard working farmer, wearing slacks and a shirt.
Joseph drove us to the bus station in Tel Aviv and we got on a bus for Haifa.

    It was nighttime, I didn't speak the language very well and Bracha didn't speak English. In Haifa the wait for the next bus would've been over an hour so she hailed a cab (or at least what I thought was a cab).
"How much to Mizrah?" she asked.
"Fourteen lirot," he replied.
"Fourteen lirot, you're crazy," she answered.
"OK," he answered, "twelve."
"Go away," she said.
    He continued to drive alongside us as we walked on the sidewalk.
"I'll give you ten," she said.
The Hebrew was simple and mostly numbers so I could follow along to some degree.
He agreed and we got in.
    I don't remember how long the drive was but there we were in the middle of the night, I was in a strange country with this strange, scary looking old lady and she is haggling with a cab driver--with a cab driver. I didn't get it,

wasn't there a meter? All I wanted was to get back on the plane and go home.

Pine trees lined the entrance to the kibbutz, and the driver said: "C'mon give me eleven lirot, an extra one, because I'm cute."

Aunt Bracha turned, handed him a ten lira note and said: "You're lucky you're getting this. You're not that cute."

You have no idea how much I wanted to bolt, but where would I go? "Ok," I thought, "I'll leave in the morning." Things looked very different in the morning, in the sunlight. I was still pretty nervous but the daytime had its effect on me.

It was the most incredible summer of my life, and I fell completely in love with my great-aunt Bracha, her husband Asher and their kids. To this day, Bracha's youngest daughter Tzofi and I are soul-mates (she's one year younger than I am). I called home and told my folks that I was staying in Israel, and they could send me all my things; I wasn't coming home.

When our son Wayne went to Israel the summer he was nine, he spent most of his time on the kibbutz as well, and was indoctrinated into the dodah Bracha way of life.

She was unique, one in a billion, she never judged and took everyone on face value. She loved you just the way you were. There are few, if any, people walking this Earth who could hold a candle to her.

My dodah Bracha died this morning, in her sleep, a month and a half after her ninety fifth birthday. She lived a very full and rich life surrounded by her life's work, her life's dreams on her Kibbutz, Kibbutz Mizrah, which she helped build and watched flourish, where she raised her family, watched them grow and watched them raise families of their own.

My father used to say that he signed a contract with G-D to live to be one hundred and twenty. "I already signed," he'd say.

We'd all sign to live the life of my son's great-great-aunt Bracha, my great-aunt Bracha, my father's aunt Bracha. L'chi B'Shalom!

What isn't in the eulogy is the love I felt for this land and the people that made it flourish. It felt as if, in America we were 'going through the motions,' and they were 'living the dream.'

We traveled all over the country, from the borders of Syria and Lebanon down through the Negev to Eilat. You couldn't get to the Western Wall (mistakenly referred to as the Wailing Wall) so I saw it from atop the Knesset. I worked the fields of Kibbutz Mizrah, getting up at four in the morning to pick melons. I milked the goats, the cows, and drank freezing cold homogenized, but not Pasteurized, milk from a forty two hundred liter vat.

I fell in love with two of my cousin's female classmates, Michal and Chava, as well as everyone else in her class. I ate Shwarma from a vendor in the streets of Jerusalem and ended up in bed with a fever of over 105. I lived on the Kibbutz along with the rest of my cousin's class and was treated as one of them.

Lenny Mandel

The toilet paper, if you could call it toilet paper, was cut up newspaper, and everybody used the shower. If the boys were taking showers the sign read 'banim'. If the girls were taking showers the sign read 'banot.' They all watched me go to take a shower with the banim sign on the door when actually the shower was being used by banot, and they all had a great laugh, even the girls; I was pretty embarrassed.

I had no fear of anything there. I walked this land, my land, with alacrity and it felt wonderful. Although I didn't practice Judaism any longer, my heart would never stray. Yup, 1962 was one hell of a summer.
And again I think-- how my life has changed.

I remember being asked to lead services on the last holy day of Passover 1993. I protested, as I didn't know the special melodies for that holiday. My protests fell on deaf ears and I led. We stood around the entrance afterward and my mother turned to me and said: "well, Lenny, if you live long enough you get to see everything!"

When my dad died in 1994 I went to synagogue three times a day. For most of that year I led the services wherever I was and I became very adept at it. One afternoon, after visiting my mother in Brooklyn, I ran over to my dad's Shul to pray.
The Rabbi asked if I would lead the afternoon service. The Shul was filled with ultra-orthodox boys, each in a white shirt, black suit and a large black hat. They all were students at the ultra-orthodox Yeshiva across the street.

From Cross To Cross

There I stood in jeans, a denim jacket with motorcycle patches all over it, and sneakers. I wore a small skullcap, the bobby pins keeping it from sliding off my head, and I had a foot long ponytail. Their mouths were hanging open in disbelief.

I finished davening and as I walked off the podium many hands stretched forth to wish me well on the beautiful service I'd just led. I walked over to one of the stunned Yeshiva boys, put my arm around his shoulder and whispered in his ear: "don't let the ponytail fool ya, kid."

Chapter 31
The Ride Home,
What I was then & Where I am Now

And now I am a Hazan, a clergyman of the Jewish faith, and like I said before, "who woulda thunk it?" I lead my synagogue in prayer as their messenger to 'The Big Guy.' It's an awesome responsibility and we start each year with the promise of wonderful things to come.

Our senses are alive with anticipation. Our nostrils are open, our taste buds await the flavor, and our ears listen to the beautiful melodies that we hope will find favor at G-D's throne. Prayer is wondrous stuff--wonderful and wondrous--and it opens up amazing things within each of us. Its power and beauty will enhance our experience every time we walk into a Shul: no matter where.

I look back and ask myself: "How the hell did this happen?" The answer is very simple; it was a phone call from Rabbi Mark Kiel the day after Rosh Hashanah 1996. That simple answer turned into a very intense educational and emotional journey for me--one that is ongoing still. It seems that their Hazan had chest pains during services and Mark wanted someone there on Yom Kippur to take over just in case.

"Not me," I said. "I need a Hazan to be my messenger on Yom Kippur. I don't want to be, nor am I qualified to be, anyone else's." He pleaded and pleaded and I finally succumbed. I didn't want to do it but I did. I bought some tapes of the Yom Kippur service, spoke to Hazan Henry Rosenblum, the dean of the Jewish Theological Seminary's Cantorial School, took a deep breath and drove to the synagogue.

Don't think that because someone goes to synagogue every year on the High Holidays he knows these intricate melodies; he doesn't, and I was no exception then. Luckily their Cantor felt fine.

Mark asked if I would daven Ne'ilah, the last hour of the day of atonement, the last chance that the Cantor, and every Jew, has to beg for G-D's mercy before He seals your fate in the 'Book of Life' for the coming year.

A Cantor spends twenty four hours fasting, and praying on Yom Kippur so that he might be worthy of pleading for his congregation during this final hour of the holiest day of the year. Their Cantor didn't want to daven Ne'ilah, and so I did.

Mark and I spoke all through the following year. He asked that I learn the intricate music and musical formulae for the morning services of both Rosh Hashanah and Yom Kippur as well as for Ne'ilah. The trustees of the synagogue wanted to hire me for the holidays.

I hired a teacher, Hazan Jacob Mendelsohn, one of the most respected conservative hazanim in America; I studied, I studied and I studied some more. It was incredible, it was overwhelming, it was scary and it was addictive. The feedback was great and Mark asked me to come back and lead services during the Feast of Weeks (Shavuot). I did--little did I know that it was an audition.

The synagogue was growing and they were looking for a younger, more assertive Hazan, with more knowledge more charisma and a beautiful voice. They offered me the position; they asked me to be their full-time Hazan.

It wasn't always cool to be up on the bimah, any bimah, leading services. That was especially true when I was young.

I remember the Rosh Hashanah when my dad led services at the Parksville Hotel in the Catskill Mountains. I must've been fourteen. There were plenty of families there and my dad asked me to learn the Torah readings for both days and chant them. Families meant other kids and I was overjoyed that I'd have other kids to play with after services ended.

It didn't happen. I was alone. I was the 'religious kid,' the outcast, but I hung-out with the band. They were kids too, seventeen to twenty, but kids nonetheless.

They liked the fact that I could sing and we hung out singing folk and rock tunes, but then a few of the girls came along and I was the odd man out again. The girls wanted to know what they were doing with me there and they shrugged their shoulders and I was gone. I could hear the giddy laughter as they close the door to their attic quarters, them inside, me outside. It sucked!

It's very different now as I lead my Congregation as their messenger in prayer to the Almighty. I'm not the odd man out anymore. No, au contraire, or as we say in Hebrew hahephech. I am still the 'religious kid,' but no longer the outcast. I'm looked up to, admired, respected and revered. It feels much better than being the outcast, believe me.

September 11, 2001 was about eight days before we were to celebrate the Jewish New Year. It seemed as if I was awake, for days after The World Trade Center devastation, writing and crying incessantly, my life and my world in limbo somewhere.

I had to let my Congregants know how I felt, and what was going on inside me, while I was davening during our High Holidays, so, again I wrote:

Rosh Hashanah, the Jewish New Year (the day that G-D writes down your fate for the coming year; on Yom Kippur, he seals the book) came. I stood on the bimah, a white shroud covering my clothing, draped in my prayer shawl, prepared to beseech G-D, for my congregation, and myself, to inscribe us all in the book of life. I would beg Him for health, prosperity and happiness for us all.

There I stood, facing the open Aron Kodesh before taking out the Torahs, and I started the familiar prayer: "Adonai, Adonai, El rachum v'chanun, erech apayim, v'rav chesed v'emet…" (G-D, Oh G-D, a gracious, compassionate, patient Lord. Full of kindness and faithfulness…), I felt you, all of you, your voices strong, as one with mine, keeping me on my feet. I felt your presence as I would hands under my arms lifting me back up and on my feet after the Grand Aleinu, and my spirit soared.

I stood there overwhelmed by the insanity of the week before. Thoughts of those I knew and lost, and more so of those I know that were lucky enough to escape, or due to whatever circumstance missed trains or had errands to run early in the morning and never made it to the office in time, echoed in my mind.

I heard myself, my head reverberating with the soulful prayer, and you, all of us, each of us, the oneness of us, beseeching G-D. Three times we chanted and then three more times we sang:
"V'ani, t'feelati, L'chah, Adonai, eyt ratzon. Elohim, b'rav chasdechah, aneyni, aneyni, be'emet yishechah" (And me, my prayer I offer to You, Oh G-D at this time of grace. Oh Lord in your abounding kindness, answer me, answer me with your true salvation).

It was a ten or twelve tissue prayer as I stood there, tears streaming down my face, thinking about a compassionate G-D, a G-D who is gracious and kind. Then, as I chanted the words, answer me, answer me (aneyni, aneyni), I was incredulous. "What am I saying," I asked myself? "Where is this compassionate, gracious, kind G-D? Huh, where is He?"

My brain raced, asking myself how dare I think of such things on such an important moment. Stop, I thought, but the words coming out of my mouth weren't making sense as my brain whirled.

It took a moment and once again I remembered Rabbi Kiel's sermon that one couldn't control his thoughts. Thoughts are thoughts. This made me smile albeit a fleeting smile, and we continued our prayers through whatever thoughts pervaded.

Near the end of Ne'ilah we chanted the "Adonai, Adonai, El rachum..." for the last time that day. It was an overwhelming twenty five plus hours of penitence, fasting and prayer, and I chanted the prayer in a whisper. There you were again, I don't know how many you were, but you were there, your whisper louder than any plaintive cry G-D heard in any congregation, anywhere in the world, this Yom Kippur day. It was another ten to twelve tissue prayer.

We ended Ne'ilah, another High Holiday Season past, and I realized that our plaintive cries, our prayers, were certainly heard by a wonderfully kind, gracious and compassionate G-D.

I realized it as I stood there on the bimah with my mother (who'd never really heard me daven before that day) sitting in the first row and my wife and son next to her, all healthy, thank G-D. "How lucky I am," I thought, "to be granted the right to pray for and with them during this awesome time."

I thanked my congregation for granting me the privilege of being their Shaliach, as most of them will never be lucky enough to feel the power of a congregation like them, as I feel their power behind me. "I know that G-D hears us through our tears as we beg and plead for his mercy," I wrote, "but I believe we've got to add a new line item to next years budget: tissues."

It is amazing; you are empowered by your own people. They trust you and, in essence, want you to "...do do--that voodoo--that you do--so well..."

From Cross To Cross

What I remember most about praying as a young child are the nigunim while wrapped in the shelter of my father's Tallit, as he swayed, back and forth and side to side, to their rhythms. Many of these are melodies that I still chant today, swaying, back and forth and side to side, feeling my father's presence. To this day the sweet aroma of him in his Tallit remains in my nostrils, taking me back to innocent times.

Now I, with my chanting, am figuratively playing the chalil, hypnotizing the King Cobra that has no choice but to sway to the combination of its plaintive sighs and the swaying motion of my body while playing it.

That's what prayer is for me, and although I don't always reach 'the heights,' I keep climbing. The cobra has no choice as he sways; the power is too great for him to resist. You too will feel the music take you, feel your bodies move and, like the cobra, be unable to resist.

"Close your eyes and come with me. Let me take you with me. Allow me to show you the way to open up your soul, to hear the music, your own music. The music only you can hear!"

I'm just completing my sixth year as Congregation B'nai Israel's Hazan, and I chastise my congregants about sneaking out of Shul before services are over.

Unlike services at most churches, services on the Sabbath are usually two and one half hours long; High Holiday services can be almost twice that.

"Just because you're gone we haven't stopped praying." I said. "Remember: it ain't over 'till the fat lady sings,' and at Congregation B'nai Israel the fat lady is me."

Route 80, I-80, droned on and on under our wheels and the towns slipped by us: Allenwood, Lewisburg (both the homes of Federal penitentiaries), Williamsport (the home of the Little League World Series). We took I-81 towards Scranton.

I recounted one of the most amazing moments I've had since being at B'nai Israel: an adult Bar/Bat Mitzvah celebration with twenty three adults celebrating their day. I use the word 'celebrate' because they already are B'nai and B'not Mitzvah. When a Jewish child turns thirteen he is responsible for his own sins and gets credit for his own good deeds. They are B'nai Mitzvah; it's an age thing not a ritual thing.

Standing before the open Torah, one's hands grasping the wooden rods on which the Torah is rolled, is awe inspiring. "It is a tree of life to them that hold fast to it..."
They recite the blessings over the Torah, sacred blessings, blessings that were against the law to recite, a crime punishable by death during our people's darkest moments in history.
How many, during the Shoah, would have chosen death if only they'd have been allowed to stand in front of our Torah and recite those words?
And what can I tell you about a Torah? Each and every Torah is hand-written. Each is done in the exact same way, with the exact same letters, in the exact same style. Each is done on parchment, each section hand-sewn to the next, and the scribe sits with quill and ink as he pens: "B'reyshit bara Elohim..." "In the beginning G-D

created..." all the way to "asher asa Moshe l'eyney kol Israel." "...which Moses wrought before the eyes of all Israel," the last lines of the Torah, the Five Books of Moses.

This Aliyah is the celebration of one's passage to adulthood from childhood, and this class worked really hard and had to put up with me as their teacher and stand-up comedian/Cantor for almost six months. There's an 'ancient' Jewish Haiku that goes: "Today I am a man, tomorrow I go back to seventh grade." Not my kidzz.

I was driving to class one night talking to my mother on the cell phone and she asked how many kids were in my class. She was right; we are all kids, some older and some younger but all kids. 'My kidzz', or as we jokingly called them 'Lenny's Kidzz', had all the same fears, all the same angst and the same butterflies our thirteen year olds have.
There will be one major difference; their parents weren't pushing them to do this, and the Rabbi never had to call their parents into his office to tell them that they weren't ready and had to work harder. No, these kidzz wanted this. No one pushed them, no one prodded them and no one made them crazy about getting the work done. They just did it.

My kidzz spoke of growing up in countries where they weren't allowed to practice Judaism and were beaten up because they were Jews. They spoke about their individual journeys and they spoke about their upbringing.
Many of the women were from very observant

homes where girls weren't even allowed on the Bimah: forget about being allowed to celebrate one's Bat Mitzvah.

One of my kidzz spoke about growing up in Romania and then Israel; she was from an observant home. She said that she felt like Yentl walking through the woods singing "...papa, can you see me, papa can you hear me..." She then spoke to her parents, both deceased, in her native tongue, Rumanian.

You can't even imagine what it felt like being there, watching her and all of my kidzz pour out their hearts. Noah probably didn't see the water rise with that much intensity. I thanked them in a letter as I was so choked with emotion that day I could hardly speak.

As each of them finished the final Blessing, the sense of relief, the feeling of release, permeated the Bimah; the glow could be seen and felt throughout the Shul. They opened up their hearts, letting their feelings flow unchecked and no one who was there will ever forget it.

It was one of the most intense and emotionally overwhelming moments of my life and I sat on the edge of the Bimah after most of them had gone: spent.
I thanked my kidzz for allowing me to help them grow and, in so doing, learn to grow myself.

As Tevye I've sung, "If I were a rich man..." many, many times. The lyric can change from "IF I were..." to "NOW I am..." because of this class, this experience.
The classes and the incredible B'nai Mitzvah weekend will remain with me as long as I live.

Epilogue—Into New Jersey

Pennsylvania became a memory as we rode through the Delaware Water Gap into New Jersey. Here was the edge of my safety net, my 'safe harbor,' and my comfort zone. We have plenty of churches in New Jersey and plenty of crosses and they never affected me the way they did on this ride.

There must have been a lot of factors at play that made this trip affect me the way it did.

Surely my immersion into the world of Judaism in a way that I never even dreamed a possibility for me was major. The way I feel when my congregants come to me for help, advice, and comfort or just to be an ear. How incredible it is knowing that I've helped someone because of my role as Cantor. How joyous it is when congregants ask me to officiate at their weddings or the weddings of their children. How emotional and moving it is for me when they come to me for solace in their darkest moments, their times of grief.

How proud I am of my son who maintains, and is very proud of his heritage and his culture, and can sit in any synagogue, anywhere in the world and pray in Hebrew.

How happy I am that he has found a wonderful girl, from a wonderful, loving and caring family and, G-D willing, they will raise children, Jewish children, who, just as our ancestors have for two thousand years, will grow up and live in this world--this Christian world.

Do not think for one moment that we do not live in a Christian world. We do; it's a fact. Our country, and believe me I sing *G-D Bless America* with pride and in full voice, is a Christian country. We celebrate--schools are closed, public buildings are closed, there is no mail, and banks are closed--New Year's Day, President's Day, Martin Luther King Day, Good Friday, Memorial Day, Independence Day, Labor Day, Columbus Day, Veteran's Day, Thanksgiving, and Christmas Day. I don't see Yom Kippur on this list so why should Good Friday or Christmas Day be on it? When did they become National, Secular holidays?
I used to work double shifts at Coney Island Hospital on Christmas and Easter so that my Christian friends could spend those days celebrating with their families.

Christ was born on December 25th? It's not possible that Christ could have been born in December and have been the Messiah--which I'm sure that by now you know I don't believe anyway.
According to the Messianic prophecy, supposedly foretold in the Old Testament, the Messiah would be born in the Hebrew month of Av, which is always during the summer. Something tells me that no one was Dreaming of a White Christmas back in those days.
I wonder if the white supremacists would sing White Christmas if they knew that a Jew wrote the song? Will ironies never cease?

From Cross To Cross

I heard a very interesting theory on why Christmas is celebrated when it is. Jews celebrated Chanukah on the 25th day of the month of Kislev. Kislev falls in December almost every year (now that we live with the Julian calendar). What is Chanukah? Chanukah is the festival of lights!

We all know the story of the Maccabees who, after entering the destroyed temple, found a flask of oil that should only have lasted one day but miraculously lasted eight days. In honor of that we light candles for eight nights.

Christmas is celebrated on the 25th of December, and how is Christmas celebrated? With lights! Christmas trees are all lit up and even many homes are ablaze with lights. The 25th of the month, be it Kislev, which is all that there was back then, or December, falls on or about the winter solstice, the shortest and therefore the darkest day of year. What better way to brighten up long dark nights than with the joyous sight of light and the warmth the candles bring (Christmas trees were lit with candles back then too). The similarities and possibilities just boggle my mind.

The towns in New Jersey sped by just as fast as the ones in Pennsylvania: Hope, Hackettstown, Mt. Olive, Hopatcong, Dover, Wharton, Rockaway and Denville. I barely noticed the signs as we rode along.

I wrote earlier about the play, "One Hundred Gates," by Tuvia Tenenbom. Near the play's end, the role that I created, Reb Beryl, stands alone on a bare stage addressing the audience about being a Jew: "... they survived all those thousands of years. No other nation in the world survived for so many years! Big nations, powerful nations; with kings and Caesars, emperors and generals--with big armies, thousands and thousands of soldiers and horses, all gone!

Only the Jewish nation, a lamb amongst seventy wolves, the oldest and smallest nation in the world, that little nation that suffered and suffers, expelled from every corner of the earth, belittled by all the nations of the world--Not one horse, not one half of a soldier, never an emperor, not a trace of a general--Only we survived..."

I hear the words, "...that little nation that suffered and suffers, expelled from every corner of the earth, belittled by all the nations of the world..." over and over and, albeit with tears in my eyes and a pain in my heart, I swell with pride.

I am a Jew, born to Jewish parents, raised to follow the traditions passed down by my ancestors for almost six thousand years. This is not a choice; it is a fact. I have blue eyes, I am balding, I have a specific genetic makeup, I am immune to some diseases and not to others, and I am a Caucasian. This list is endless and these are facts, not choices.

I am very proud to be a Jew and prouder still to have been able to impart this to my son knowing that he will do the same to his.

I stand tall and proud at the lectern of my synagogue praying for my congregation: a leader in the community. It's my heritage, it's my right and I'll be damned if I'll let anyone try to take it away again.

From Cross To Cross

I look in the mirror now and I like what I see, and that wasn't always the case. It's not the physical, it's what's going on inside me that I see and that I like.

There are plenty of things I've done that I wish I could change, that I wish I could take back, things that I'm not proud of; I can't, but those were choices not absolutes: wrong choices, but choices nonetheless. Absolutes are things that you are born with, things about which you have no choice. "Ya gotta dance with the one that brung ya, don't ya?"

When the Nazis came for the Jews, they took all the Jews, even those that had converted long before the threat of extermination. The final solution: the eradication of the Jews, and why not; they were the bane of the world's existence, the cause of everything evil in the world. Maybe that's why all the crosses and all the churches affected me the way they did.

Do not think for a moment that I believe that anti-Semitism is only perpetrated by gentiles. It is actually incredible how much anti-Semitism we have to deal with from our own people; from other Jews. Whether it is fear that someone will think that they are of the same ilk or whether it's embarrassment, I don't care. This story puts it into perspective for me.

> *There's a woman, a snotty Jewish woman, sitting on a bus directly across from a Hasid.*
> *After a few minutes of fidgeting in her seat she faces him directly and says:* "*You Hasidim are an embarrassment to us.*

You dress as if you live in the middle ages, you never bathe, you smell, you breed like rabbits and you let your children run amok.
Why don't you get over that nonsense and come join the rest of the world in the 21st century?"
The man looks at her, smiles and says: "I'm sorry madam but I'm not a Hasid, I'm Amish!"
She stops in mid sentence and says; "Oh, you know, it is so beautiful the way your people stay true to your customs."

In the film The Unsinkable Molly Brown, Molly is snubbed by the nouveau riche society in Denver. She's a bumpkin who got lucky and struck gold, and they want no part of her or her family. She goes over to Europe and hangs out with royalty who adore her, and they spend hours and hours having a wonderful time.

Molly, although thoroughly at ease and enjoying herself with her new friends asks them why they accept her unconditionally and the society folk in Denver shun her.

One of the nobles turns to her and says: "It's because they are only one generation away from where you are."

To deny one's heritage is to murder all that came before you; that's what I say.

I heard a story about a young Jewish boy who was learning the 23rd Psalm. His father sat with him and taught him the Psalm: "The Lord is my Shepherd I shall not want…"

About a week later the father asked the son if he'd learned the 23rd Psalm by heart yet.

The boy nodded and said; "Yes, papa, but I've made a correction."

Controlling his anger the father asked his son to recite the Psalm, which the young boy did.

He recited: "The Lord is my Shepherd, what else could I want?"

We turned onto route 280; we were about seven miles from home. As we stopped at the red light at the end of the ramp of our exit, a convertible sports car passed in front of us--my convertible sports car. There, they were, our son and future daughter-in-law, tooling down the street in it.

We saw each other at the same time and our faces lit up as the four of us waved. They pulled over to wait for us and escorted us to the house.

We were home!

I would be remiss if I didn't close with one of my dad's favorite stories.

Isaac and Vincent were very close friends, growing up together in Brooklyn. Each went to seminary; Vincent became a Priest and Isaac a Rabbi.
Isaac took a job as the Rabbi of a small shul, a shteibel, in Borough Park and one day the phone rang in his office:
"Hello, is this Ike?" the voice on the line asked.
"Yes, Vinnie, it's me how are you?" he replied."
"I'm the Priest at St. Anthony's in the city," he said.
Ike says: "So what!"
"Wadda you mean, so what, are you still in that little shteibel?" he asked.
"Yup," Ike answered, and hung up.
Three years later the phone rang in Ike's office again:
"Hello, is this Ike?" the voice on the line asked.
"Yes, Vinnie, it's me how are you?" he replied."
"Ike, I was made the Monsignor at St. Anthony's," he said.
Ike replied: "So what!"
"Wadda you mean, so what, are you still in that little shteibel?" he asked.
"Yup," Ike answered again, and, once again, hung up.
Ten years went by and again the phone rang in Ike's office: "Hello, Ike?" the voice on the line asked.
"Yes, this is Ike. How are you Vince?" he replied.
"Ike, I'm a Bishop in the Cleveland diocese," he said.
Ike replied: "So what!"

"Wadda you mean, so what, are you still in that little shteibel?" he asked once more.
"Yup," Ike answered again, and, once again, hung up.
Vincent was made a Cardinal and lived in Italy at the College of Cardinals.
The Pope died and black smoke rose from the chimney for a week and then, finally, white smoke.
Once again the phone rang in Brooklyn: "Ike," the voice on the line spoke, "it's Vince, Ike. I called to see how you are doing and to let you know that I am the Pope, the Pope, Ike."
There was a momentary silence on the line and Ike spoke: "So what," he declared.
"I'm the Pope," Vincent said, "the Pope. Wadda you want me to do be Jesus Christ?"
Ike smiled and said: "well, one of our boys made it!"

THE END

GLOSSARY OF JEWISH TERMS

Aleph	(A–the first letter of the Hebrew alphabet)
Aleph Bet	(The Hebrew alphabet).
Aliyah	(To go up onto the Bimah to be honored)
Aron Kodesh	(The Holy Ark–where the Torah is kept)
Ashkenazi	(One of Eastern European descent)
Ashkenazim	(Plural of Ashkenazi)
Banim	(Boys)
Banot	(Girls)
Baqshert	(Pre-ordained–meant to be)
Bar Mitzvah	(Son of the Commanments)
Bat Mitzvah	(Daughter of ...)
Bekisheh	(Long coat worn by ultra-orthodox Jews)
Belzer	(From the city of Belz, Poland)
Bimah	(The stage)
Birkat Hamazon	(Grace after meals)
B'nai	(Sons of)
B'not	(Daughters of)
Bubby	(Grandmother)
Cantor	(Messenger of the congregation in prayer to G-D)
Chagall	(Famous Jewish artist–Marc Chagall)
Chanukah	(Festival of lights)

Chai	(Hebrew for LIFE)
Chag Sameach	(Happy Holiday—the words are written holiday happy)
Chalil	(An instrument known as a Recorder)
Chalutzim	(Pioneers)
Cheder	(school)
Cheshvan	(A month in the Hebrew calendar)
Charoset/choroutzes	(A mixture of apples, nuts and sweet wine, this is eaten during the Seder on Passover)
Chutzpah	(Nerve—balls—gall)
Cohanim	(Priests)
Daven/davening	(Pray/praying)
Dodah	(Hebrew for aunt)
Erev Shabbat	(Eve of Sabbath)
Frumkeit	(Religiousness—being observant)
Galicia	(A province of the former Austro-Hungarian Empire)
Galitzianer	(One who comes from Galicia)
Gartel	(the braided, fringed belt that the ultra-orthodox wear to separate the cerebral and the impure)
Gefilte fish	(A combination of Carp and Pike—every one prepares it differently)
Gimmel	(Third letter of the Hebrew alphabet)
Glayzele	(A little glass of...)
Gut Moid	(Good interim day)
Gut Shabbes	(Good Sabbath)
Gut Voch	(Good Week)
Gut Yohr	(Good Year)
Gut Yontif	(Good Holiday—happy holiday)
Haggadah	(The book that is read during the seders every Passover)

HaShomer Hatzair	(The young guard-a Socialist organization)
Hasid	(Follower of)
Hasidic	(One who follows the teachings)
Havdalah	(Prayer that separates the Holy days from other days)
Hazan	(Cantor)
Kaddish	(Prayer recited Sanctifying G-D's Name)
Kibbutz	(Communal farm)
Kiddush	(Blessing over wine)
Kipah	(Skullcap)
Knesset	(parliament)
L'Chayim	(To life)
L'chi B'Shalom	(go in peace)
Latkes	(Potato pancakes)
Levites	(Descendants of the Tribe of Levi–Jacob's third son)
Lirot	(Israeli currency)
Litvak	(Jews of old Lithuania)
Luchot HaBrit	(The Tablets of the Covenant--The Ten Commandments)
Maccabee(s)	(Hebrew for hammer(s)–the family which defeated Antiochus)
Magen David	(mistakenly referred to as a Star of David--or Jewish Star--it means shield of David as this was the star painted on his shield when King David went into battle--or so the story goes)
Mandlen	(Almonds–when used in conjunction with soup, means soup nuts)

Matzos	(Unleavened bread primarily eaten on Passover)
Midrash	(Interpretation or exegesis)
Mikvah	(Ritual bath)
Mincha	(the afternoon service)
Minyan	(The quorom of ten Jews required for communal prayer)
Mitzvah	{mitzvot is plural}(commandment or deed)
Moed Sameach	(Happy interim day–some festivals have regular days between holy days-these are called interim days)
Motzi	(Blessing over bread)
Ne'ilah	(The prayers comprising the last hour of the Day of Atonement)
Nigunim	(melodies)
Nu	(C'mon already)
Payes	(Sidelocks)
Pogrom(s)	(Massive, violent attack(s) on Jews)
Rebbe	(Spiritual leader, much more than just a Rabbi)
Rosh Hashanah	(New Year)
Rugelach	(A pastry–cookie)
Schlep	(To drag along)
Schwarma	(Pressed meats on a standing skewer)
Seder	(Literally means order–also the service at the table on Passover)
Sephardic	(Descendant of Middle Eastern, Spanish, Greek or Turkish Jews)
Sephardim	(Plural of Sephardic)
Shabbat	(Sabbath)
Shabbat HaMalka	(Sabbath Queen)

Shabbat Shalom	(Peaceful Sabbath–means– May you have...)
Shaliach	(messenger)
Shanah Tovah	(Good Year--means--- May you have...)
Shavua Tov	(Good week--means--- May you have...)
Shechinah	(The Holy Presence)
Shiva	(Seven day mourning period after a loved one dies)
Shmuck	(Penis [literally]--means–idiot)
Shoah	(The Holocaust)
shtender	(The lectern)
Shtetl	(Village)
Shtetlach	(The little shtetls--villages)
Shtraymel	(A hat circled in mink)
Shul	(Synagogue)
Simchas Torah	(Holiday celebrating the Torah)
Sukkah	(A hut in which people lived during the harvest)
Tallis (or Tallit)	(Prayer Shawl)
Talmud	(Jewish law and ethics)
Tevye	(The father in Fiddler on the Roof)
Torah	(The scroll containing The Five Books of Moses)
Tuchas	(Rear end--butt--ass)
Tzitzis	(Fringed garment)
Vantz	(Bedbug–idiomatically means one who gets into everything)
Yahrtzeit	(Year's time–anniversary)
Yarmulke	(Skullcap)
Yiddishkeit	(Jewishness)
Yiddlach	(Jews)

Lenny Mandel

Yom Kippur   (The Day of Atonement)
Zeide   (Grandfather)

GLOSSARY OF BIKER TERMS

1% ers	(Outlaws)
Ape-hangers	(Very high handlebars)
Boogie	(Ride quickly without stopping or sightseeing)
Brain-bucket	(Tiny helmet worn by bikers to get around helmet laws)
Chopper	(Motorcycle that has been stripped down to bare essentials)
Crash bars	(Engine guards–they take the early shock in case you go down)
Do-rag	(The cloth that many bikers wear on their hair-looks like what your grandmother wore when she worked around the house)
Flathead	(Type of Harley Davidson engine from the early to mid 40s)
FLHS	(Type of Harley Davidson)
Harley Ultra	(Type of Harley Davidson)
Highway pegs	(Footpegs attached as far forward on your bike allowing you to stretch your legs on a long ride)
H.O.G.	(Harley Owners Group)
Ink	(Tattoos)
Kuryakin	(Company specializing in motorcycle paraphernalia)
Limp it in	(Drive slowly)

Lenny Mandel

Panhead	(Type of Harley Davidson engine from the late 40s to 1965)
Pipes	(Exhaust pipes)
Ride	(Motorcycle)
Road King	(Type of Harley Davidson)
Scoot	(Motorcycle)
Stock	(The way a motorcycle comes from the factory)
Stroker	(Changing where the piston is connected which adds power)
Suicide clutch	(A foot clutch—only seen on motorcycles for a very short time)
Tank shift	(This shifter is a stick shift on the tank)
The lowers	(On the crash bars protecting ones legs from the elements)
Thumbscrew	(Literally a screw that you turn to hold the throttle in place—a rudimentary form of cruise control)
Thunder-Headers	(The exhaust system manufactured by Thunderheader)
Tricked out	(With many extras)
Tweaked the throttle	(Accelerated)
Two up	(Riding with a passenger sitting behind you)
Whooping on the throttle	(Accelerating rapidly—pedal to the metal so to speak)

Printed in the United States
35629LVS00004B/106-204